The Circular Economy

D0322718

A circular economy seeks to rebuild capital, whether this is financial, manufactured, human, social or natural, and offers opportunities and solutions for all organisations. This book, written by Walter Stahel, who is widely recognised as one of the key people who formulated the concept of the circular economy, is the perfect introduction for anyone wanting to quickly get up to speed with this vitally important topic for ensuring sustainable development. It sets out a new framework that refines the concept of a circular economy and how it can be applied at industrial levels.

This concise book presents the key themes for busy managers and policy-makers and some of the newest thinking on the topic of the circular economy from one of the leading thinkers in the field. Practical examples and case studies with real-life data are used to elucidate the ideas presented within the book.

Walter R. Stahel is the Founder-Director of the Product-Life Institute (Switzerland), the oldest established consultancy in Europe devoted to developing sustainable strategies and policies. He is Visiting Professor in the Department of Engineering and Physical Sciences, University of Surrey, and a full member of the Club of Rome. He was awarded degrees of Doctor honoris causa by the University of Surrey (2013) and l'Université de Montréal (2016).

The Circular Economy
A User's Guide

Walter R. Stahel

with a foreword by Dame Ellen MacArthur

edited by the Ellen MacArthur Foundation

Routledge
Taylor & Francis Group

LONDON AND NEW YORK

First published 2019
by Routledge
2 Park Square, Milton Park, Abingdon, Oxon OX14 4RN

and by Routledge
711 Third Avenue, New York, NY 10017

Routledge is an imprint of the Taylor & Francis Group, an informa business

© 2019 Walter R. Stahel

British Library Cataloguing-in-Publication Data
A catalogue record for this book is available from the British Library

Library of Congress Cataloging-in-Publication Data
Names: Stahel, Walter R., author.
Title: The circular economy : a user's guide / Walter R. Stahel.
Description: New York : Routledge, 2019. | Includes bibliographical references and index.
Identifiers: LCCN 2019002504| ISBN 9780367200145 (hardback) | ISBN 9780367200176 (pbk.) | ISBN 9780429259203 (ebook)
Subjects: LCSH: Sustainable development. | Environmental policy. | Natural resources--Environmental aspects.
Classification: LCC HC79.E5 S6693 2019 | DDC 338.9/27--dc23
LC record available at https://lccn.loc.gov/2019002504

ISBN: 978-0-367-20014-5 (hbk)
ISBN: 978-0-367-20017-6 (pbk)
ISBN: 978-0-429-25920-3 (ebk)

Typeset in Bembo
by Taylor & Francis Books

Contents

Illustrations

Table

Figures

Acknowledgements

The author thanks
  Ian Banks
  Mike Harrison
  Nathalie Vercruysse
  Ken Webster
  for critical comments and reviews of the manuscripts,
  Graham Pritchard for the 'reinvention' of my graphics,
  Andrew Clifton for researching and providing the book cover picture,
  Lena Gravis for the editing work,
  Rolls-Royce plc. for its courtesy in providing the author with a photograph
for the book cover, which symbolises the beauty of product use and techno-
logical progress in a circular and performance economy, putting function over
fashion.

Note from the author

This book is a tool box for behavioural analysis; it is not a textbook of economics, molecular biology or material sciences, even if these disciplines are important to understand circularity.

This book appeals to common sense and attempts to explain the circular economy for those who see it as black box; it will therefore challenge experts' knowledge. The working title of the book has been for a long time *Circular economy for beginners*.

Foreword

No one has done more to make the case for the transition to a circular economy than my friend Walter Stahel. Not only because he has been doing it longer and with more care and humility than anyone else, but first and foremost because his words have proved to be just what our changing times need. His strength, his persistence, and a lifetime of reflection built on observing the worlds of business, design and manufacturing have culminated in this short book. Every page contains either something worth learning or an expression that will be picked up and shared. Books of that ilk are rare.

Walter set out to create a beginner's guide, but his effort exceeded that objective, resulting in a discourse that brings clarity and precision to the sometimes-misconstrued concept of the circular economy.

For more than 40 years, Walter has been developing this idea, constantly renewing himself and exploring many paths. So, what does this this book reveal that we do not already know? It seems to me that for the first time Walter places the concept of circular economy in its historical context, and in doing so gives it greater depth and legitimacy. From a strategy to address resource scarcity, the circular economy has become an industrial model of development 'appealing to individuals as the most desirable and sustainable option'.

Of course, the Performance Economy occupies a prominent place in this book, which is to be expected from the founding father of the concept. Walter insists on the importance of the notion of caring as 'a requirement in the Performance Economy which is based on a shared used of objects'. Indeed, he stresses that the circular industrial economy overall relies both on caring and on trust.

Other concepts appear in this book and deserve attention, for example the idea of recovering molecules and atoms and reusing them at high levels of purity. A challenging new dimension of circular activities to be sure, but one full of the promise of economic and environmental benefits. There is no doubt that these new developments will be the subject of passionate debate among circular economy experts – a group that is far more numerous than 40 years ago.

Reflecting on his work to date, Walter concludes that while he has provided useful descriptive tools, he may have failed to motivate people to start the necessary transition – that 'longing for the sea' he expresses using Saint-Exupéry's words. I would beg to differ and encourage him to consider that the current enthusiasm for the circular economy idea owes a great deal to his influence.

Dame Ellen MacArthur

Introduction: Circular by nature

This book gives the reader an idea of the opportunities of the circular economy (CE), by describing circularity, its history, structure and mechanisms.

Circularity is the principle governing nature and a circular society, the latter enabled early mankind to overcome a scarcity of resources, people and skills by making the best use of the natural resources available; sharing and reuse were a necessity and the norm. When a castle became superfluous through political changes or a cathedral redundant, their structure was dismantled and the stones used to build new houses or bridges. This circular society has been man's best friend, omnipresent and discreet, for a long time, driven by scarcity.

Circularity has been ubiquitous and omnipresent throughout the history of planet Earth, in two distinctively different forms:

NATURE: water and material cycles are the norm, some unpredictable like weather, others periodic like tidal cycles. Nature is governed by a self-organised system of virtuous material cycles where organic waste is food and remuneration for others. The "labour" to do this is provided by trillions of bacteria, insects and other small animals, free of charge and untaxed; natural processes are not subjected to constraints of time, money or culture, nor rules or liability; nature has no master plan, no events are perceived as negative.

MANKIND: A "circular society" in the sense of exchange has been present throughout the history of mankind. Individuals created goods and tools from natural resources, such as wood or stone, for their own use and for exchange in a barter economy. Then, craftsmen appeared, using their skills to create goods for others, explore new materials like metals and ceramics and repair broken objects as a service to their owners. This evolution was driven by human desire for a better quality of life and by individual initiatives.

Human capital—people, their skills and creativity combined with a caring attitude—is the basis of this circular society. Caring for and sharing of stocks—natural, cultural, manufactured and social capitals—has been the engine of the circular society of the past and the basis of our sustainable future.

This book focuses on the opportunities of MANKIND, a circular economy of manufactured—man made—objects and materials, its potential and drivers, as well as its risks and limitations.

The circular economy evolves through two major shifts: from necessity to solution of last resort to default option

or from a circular society of necessity due to people's poverty or a scarcity of resources, to a circular economy in a society of abundance as a solution of last resort to overcome devastating waste problems, and finally to a circular industrial economy as default option, appealing to individuals as the most desirable and sustainable option.

The last step is the most challenging one; the French pilot-poet Antoine de Saint-Exupéry (1900–1945) touched upon this kind of challenge in his unfinished book *Citadelle*[1]:

> *Quand tu veux construire un bateau, ne commence pas par rassembler du bois, couper des planches et organiser des ouvriers, mais crée la pente vers la mer, réveille au sein des hommes le désir de la mer grande et large.*

> When you want to build a ship, do not begin by gathering wood, cutting boards and organising work gangs, but rather create the longing for the sea, awaken within men the desire for the vast and endless sea.

The shift to a Circular industrial economy therefore can be accelerated by motivating

- individuals to dream of happiness beyond ownership,[2,3]
- owner-users of goods, and economic actors owning and operating objects, to care for the stocks of objects and materials in their possession, and
- policymakers to draft framework conditions which create Saint-Exupéry's longing, and self-propels the shift to a circular economy and other sustainable solutions.

Notes

1 Antoine Marie Jean-Baptiste Roger, comte de Saint-Exupéry. This is an approximate quote as Saint-Exupéry wrote about this challenge on several occasions in his book.
2 In Buddhism, happiness is defined as "The sum of your belongings divided by the sum of your wants". Decreasing your wants increases your happiness.
3 Aristotle stated that real wealth lies in the use of goods, not ownership – 2000 years ago.

Bibliography

Saint-Exupéry, Antoine (1948) *Citadelle*. Gallimard, Paris

1 The circular economy, roots and context

Circularity has been the guiding principle of nature since the very beginning. Early man lived in a circular society of scarcity and dearth, a non-monetary circular society driven by necessity, which still exists in many industrially less developed regions of the world. The objective of the circular economy is to maintain the values, and manage stocks, of assets, from natural, cultural, human, manufactured to financial stocks. People in the circular economy of scarcity are driven by need, no other motivation needed, and it is the most sustainable post-industrial economy business model available.

1.1 History

The circular economy always had the objective to optimise the use of objects, not their production; to preserve the use value of stocks of objects, components and molecules at their highest utility and value levels; and to profitably manage these stocks in competition with other economic options. Natural cycles, by contrast, have no purpose or objective, no monetary or cultural constraints.

The historic development of the circular economy as an accumulative process over time is shown in Table 1.1. Today, various forms of circularity, circular society and circular economy exist in parallel, intertwined and in competition with the linear industrial economy.

Circularity has been the guiding principle of nature since the very beginning. The same molecules have been used, dismantled and reused in cycles, a giant LEGO, enabling fauna and flora to adapt to changing conditions by developing a growing biodiversity. But circularity in nature cannot recognise manufactured objects and objects made from manufactured materials as "bad": micro-plastics in the oceans will be eaten by fish, which may become food eaten by people. Similarly, salt harvested from the sea through evaporation, which gourmets prefer to rock salt, contains micro-plastics; nothing is ignored in nature. Mankind has a moral obligation to retain the control of manufactured materials and objects, which nature cannot decompose, in its own interest.

Early man lived in a circular society of scarcity and dearth and made the best use of available natural resources and existing objects in order to survive, as expressed in the old New England maxim:

Use it up, wear it out, make it do or do without.

Table 1.1 Evolution of parallel phases of circularity

	CIRCULARITY	CIRCULAR SOCIETY	INDIVIDUAL CIRCULAR SOCIETY	CIRCULAR INDUSTRIAL ECONOMY (CIE)
TIMELINE				
STARTED BY	FOREVER	MANKIND	INDUSTRIAL MAN	INDUSTRIAL FIRMS
DRIVERS	NATURE	BELIEFS, CULTURE, TRADITION (AMISH)	NECESSITY, GOOD HUSBANDRY	MAINTAINING VALUES, EFFICIENCY IN USE
ACTORS		GROUPS	INDIVIDUALS	FLEET MANAGERS
EXAMPLES	WATER CYCLE, CARBON CYCLE	SHARED USE, COMMONS, TRADITIONAL DRESS, PUBLIC LIBRARIES,	SENSE OF CARING, REUSE OF GARMENTS, COLLECTORS' ITEMS, MAINTENANCE	SERVICE-LIFE EXTENSION, REMANUFACTURING OF GOODS & COMPONENTS, RECOVERING MOLECULES
VALUES	IMMATERIAL	NON-MONETARY	PERSONAL	MONETARY
IN CONTROL	NATURE	OWNER–USERS	OWNER–USERS	OWNER-MANAGERS
CIRCULAR ACTIVITIES	FORESTRY, AGRICULTURE	SHARING SCHEMES	DO-IT-YOURSELF, REPAIR CRAFTSMEN	RENTAL SCHEMES, LEASING, EU RAIL POOL
RANGE	GLOBAL	LOCAL	LOCAL	OBJECTS REGIONAL, MOLECULES GLOBAL

Circular societies driven by necessity still exist in many industrially less developed regions of the world.

Non-monetary sharing was an integral part of a circular society of necessity – witness the Commons in many villages hundred years ago. Repair cafés are a modern form of the sharing society: people with broken objects regularly meet people with expert knowledge and the necessary tools to repair objects and discuss life. A sharing society makes sense for working people at all levels:

> initiatives in science encourage pooling surplus reagents, sharing equipment or keeping better tabs on lab chemicals to avoid duplication. These exercises are about helping science as much as helping the planet. They free up resources that can be applied for scientific purposes.
>
> (James 2018)

Wasted materials are also wasted money.

The development of skills and capabilities gradually allowed humankind to better exploit the available natural resources; social and cultural innovation, new tools and technologies further improved its quality of life. Two hundred and fifty years ago, the industrial revolution allowed people in many regions to overcome scarcities of food, shelter and clothing, by exploiting the opportunities of a linear industrial economy, but today the downsides of the linear industrial economy are overwhelming.

The downsides of the linear industrial economy are today one of the drivers of a shift towards the circular industrial economy detailed in the following chapters of this book.

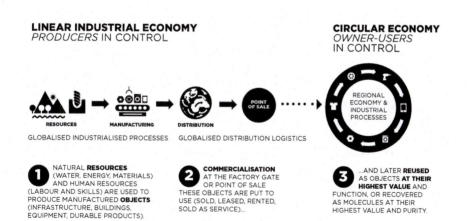

Figure 1.1 Situating the linear economy, the circular economy and the actors in control

1.2 The realm of the circular economy

The circular economy is the most sustainable post-production business model. It uses natural, human, cultural and manufactured stocks to improve the ecologic, social and economic factors that make up sustainability. But the circular economy is not the only smart and green strategy available.

'Greening of Industry' concepts (Saikku *et al.* 2015), like Industrial Ecology and Industrial Symbioses, involve cascades of reusing wastes from production processes within the linear industrial economy. These concepts manage production waste, reduce the environmental impairment and increase the economic efficiency of production. But their aim is not to maximise the use of physical assets: closed loops of water or heat would often be more resource efficient than a cascading use of excess heat or water. Yet to reduce production costs, the linear industrial economy also uses such circular economy strategies as repair and preventive maintenance services for its production machinery and equipment. By hardening the steel blades of buckets used in mining, for instance, it reduces down-time and wear and tear, extends the overall service-life of the buckets and reduces production costs.

In the late twentieth century, efforts started to green industry. A number of new fields of research arose, with the aim to optimise the supply chain of production and value added up to the point of sale.

In fact, industrial waste is a double financial loss, in the form of resources lost and waste management costs, both for energy and materials. It is therefore amazing that economic actors in the linear industrial economy need to be motivated to prevent waste.

Waste prevention is also a cultural issue because waste can be regarded as economic inefficiency. To promote waste prevention in countries, which are proud of their production efficiency, like Japan, it can be sufficient to point out to managers that waste is inefficient and they are therefore behaving in an un-Japanese way − a near insult.

The efforts of greening industry have several origins, objectives and inventors:

- Industrial ecology is a young science that studies industrial systems with the goal of finding ways to lessen their environmental impact, to learn how industries can use industrial ecology to reduce their consumption of natural resources and generate less waste.[1] Thomas Graedel was one of its founders. This concept can be extended to end-of-pipe sectors, such as municipal waste water treatment plants recovering phosphorous, which can be reused as fertiliser.
- Industrial symbiosis is an association between two or more industrial facilities or companies in which the wastes or by-products of one become the raw materials for another, in a linear cascading approach; its lighthouse example is the Kalundborg eco-industrial park. Pure gypsum is a waste product from coal-fired power stations which can be directly used as a

resource by plaster board manufacturers instead of natural gypsum. Industrial symbioses is vulnerable to structural change; if plasterboard manufacturers are forced to take back their products, they may give preference to reuse their used products instead of the gypsum waste from power stations.

- Industrial metabolism was proposed by Robert Ayres in analogy to the biological metabolism as 'the whole integrated collection of physical processes that convert raw materials and energy, plus labour, into finished products and wastes'.
- Cleaner production is a preventive, company-specific environmental protection initiative. It is intended to minimise waste and emissions and maximise product output.

The construction industry is the biggest buyer of resources, and has become a leading greening industry: the reuse of materials instead of disposal is today the preferred option in most new infrastructure projects.

> Building the new 57 kilometres long Gotthard rail tunnel – the world's longest – produced the equivalent of five Giza pyramids of mining waste,[2] which were used as raw material to build the new (infra)structure of the project, including spray-concrete for the tunnel itself. Of the 28 million tonnes of rock excavated, 15 kilograms were delivered to the Swiss post office, ground into fine powder and, using a special paint, integrated into a special issue of postal stamps named 'Gottardo 2016'. The hot water of sources inside the tunnel is captured and used by a new fish farming industry near the tunnel entrance – a cascading use of natural resources (NZZ 2016).
> Similarly, 98 percent of the seven million tonnes of material excavated in building the new Elizabeth Line in London has been reused in quarries, a golf course, a farm and nature reserves along the river Thames (Explore 2018).

Other approaches define a circular economy by using different criteria, such as loops or policy areas.

The famous butterfly diagram developed by the Ellen MacArthur Foundation, for example, takes a resource view and distinguishes between loops of the Biosphere (Foster 2018), such as regenerative agriculture (circularity in Table 1.1) and loops of the Technosphere, the circular industrial economy (Ellen MacArthur Foundation 2013).

Some policymakers see similarities in the policy areas between bioeconomy and the circular industrial economy of manufactured objects and molecules. However, according to a 2018 European Environment Agency Report (EEA 2018), 'the increasing demand for food, feed, biomaterials and bioenergy resources could worsen the present overexploitation of natural resources'.

Goods destined for consumption, such as food, feed, energy and water, which cannot be resold or used a second time (and thus are unproductive in the sense of Adam Smith), are not in the focus of this book. One cannot eat a sandwich twice, but it makes sense to 'close the loop' by feeding food leftovers to pigs, or to transform food waste into biogas (methane). But these are linear cascading processes to prevent waste, the value of stock (food), however, is lost for a later productive use.

This book renounces to look into this rapidly expanding domain of the bioeconomy, which encompasses the production of renewable biological resources and their conversion into food, feed, bio-based products and bio-energy. Bioeconomy (in the definition of the EU) includes agriculture, fisheries, food and pulp and paper production, as well as parts of the chemical, biotechnical and energy industries.[3]

The bioeconomy focuses on a more efficient industrial use of natural capital, but its economic characteristics resemble more the linear than the circular industrial economy. Most of its products cannot be reused, and molecules can only exceptionally be recovered from waste streams, once appropriate technologies will have been developed. Recovering phosphorus in waste water treatment plants, for example, has been done in pilot projects. Often, these can be justified for reasons of pollution prevention but questions remain over the economic viability. And the question arises if prevention policies in the use of phosphorous would not be more sustainable than the recovery through end-of-pipe waste management.

Nevertheless, there are some overlapping topics, referred to as 'junctions', which can help to guide research into the most promising fields, and therefore should be on the radar of policymakers (Foresight 2015).

1.3   What distinguishes the circular economy from the linear industrial economy?

The circular industrial economy manages stocks of manufactured assets, such as infrastructure, buildings, vehicles, equipment and consumer goods, to maintain their value and utility as high as possible for as long as possible; and stocks of resources at their highest purity and value.

This model contrasts with the linear industrial economy in that its objectives are to maintain value (not to create value added), to optimise stock management (not flows) and to increase the efficiency of using goods (not of producing goods) (see Figure 1.1).

The linear industrial economy stops, and the circular economy starts, at the point of sale or the factory gate, where ownership and liability for goods are sold from manufacturers to owner-users and after which owner-users have the option to optimise – or not to optimise – the use of goods as assets in concentric loops of reuse, repair and remanufacture. Owner-users' decisions can be based on ecologic, economic, social or cultural factors and are open to outside influences, such as education, peer or herd behaviours, marketing and ethical appeals.

An asset management to maintain the value and utility of stocks for the longest period of time is the key feature that distinguishes the circular industrial economy from the flow management of supply chains to create instant value added of the linear industrial economy. The circular industrial economy introduces an attitude of 'caring' and the 'factor time' into economics and society. Often, it is the case that society is as wasteful with knowledge as it is with manufactured objects and material resources: the knowledge of the past often dies with the knowledgeable people. Museums and libraries can preserve the artefacts created by knowledge, but hardly the knowledge itself, which integrates the accumulated experience of 'hit and miss', the successes and failures gained in applying the knowledge.

Waste prevention is part of optimising the use of objects in the circular industrial economy, whereas waste management is the final phase of the linear industrial economy of 'take, make, SELL, consume and dispose'.

If and when disposal costs become relevant for producers of the linear industrial economy, for instance through an Extended Producer Liability, producers have a strong financial incentive to prevent waste and liability costs from end-of-service-life objects. Shifting from flow to stock management becomes then a preferred strategy for producers to reduce their (life-cycle) costs and maximise their profits. An Extended Producer Liability may be the most powerful tool for policymakers to promote such a shift, to making the circular industrial economy the default option for economic actors, individuals and policymakers.

The circular economy employs local small-scale processes (craftsmen, Do-It-Yourself and repair cafés) to extend the service-life of manufactured objects; the circular industrial economy develops regional industrial processes (remanufacturing workshops and factories) to achieve the same objectives.

This contrasts with activities to recover atoms and molecules of end-of-service-life objects, where industrial processes based on economies of scale are the norm. As a general rule, the higher the purity of the recovered materials has to be, the smaller the batch volumes of each recovery process will be. Using conventional technology, this activity will need to be global in order to achieve economies of scale. Innovation into small-volume processes to recover atoms and molecules would therefore greatly increase the environmental feasibility of the processes, by shortening the transport distances between collection and processing.

In both cases, existing manufacturing technologies and processes are of little help.

Manufacturing technologies also have limited influence on some flourishing areas of the circular economy where culture, skills and a high personal motivation of craftsmen come together, such as violin makers. The craftsmen of this profession not only play, repair and remanufacture string instruments; their pride is often also in building new instruments. This is a labour of love, not of profit maximisation; witness the activities of '*luthiers sans frontiers*' taking their knowledge to less developed countries,[4] and also an example of the invisible and quiet nature of the circular economy (see Chapter 6).

Notes

1 Wikipedia's definition.
2 Altogether, the new tunnel system consists of 152 km of tunnels and produced 28.2 million tonnes of evacuated rock.
3 The bioeconomy comprises those parts of the economy that use renewable biological resources from land and sea – such as crops, forests, fish, animals and micro-organisms – to produce food, materials and energy. https://ec.europa.eu/research/bioeconomy/index.cfm, accessed 15 January 2019. On 20 July 2018, the European Commission launched the new Bioeconomy Knowledge Centre to better support EU and national policymakers and stakeholders with science-based evidence in this field. The platform will not primarily generate knowledge, but will collect, structure and make accessible knowledge from a wide range of scientific disciplines and sources on the bioeconomy, the sustainable production of renewable biological resources and their conversion into valuable products. The Knowledge Centre is being created by the Commission's in-house science service, the Joint Research Centre, in cooperation with Directorate-General for Research and Innovation. https://ec.europa.eu/research/bioeconomy/index.cfm?pg=policy&lib=observatory, accessed 15 January 2019.
4 www.lsf-uk.org, accessed 20 December 2018.

References

Ellen MacArthur Foundation (2013) *A new dynamic, effective business in a circular economy.* Ellen MacArthur Foundation Publishing, Cowes.

European Environment Agency (EEA) Report (2018) EEA, Copenhagen.

Explore Paddington (Spring/Summer/Spring/Summer2018) *On the right track.* Pamphlet, p. 17.

Foresight (2015) The junction of health, environment and the bioeconomy: Foresight and implication for European Research & Innovation Policies. DG for Research and Innovation, Directorate A, Unit A6. Publications Office of the European Union, Luxembourg.

Foster, William (2018) There's a jungle in your bed. *Nature*, vol. 563, p. 31.

James, Peter (2018) Director of S-Lab, a UK initiative based in London that promotes sustainable lab practices, quoted in *Nature*, vol. 554, p. 265.

NZZ (2016) Aus dem Berg in den See und anderswohin. *Neue Zürcher Zeitung*, 24 May, p. 7.

Saikku, Laura, Antikainen, Riina, Droste, Nils, Pitkänen, Kati, Loiseau, Eleonore, Hansjürgens, Bernd, Kuikman, Peter, Leskinen, Pekka and Thomsen, Marianne (2015) Implementing the green economy in a European context: Lessons learned from theories, concepts and case studies. PEER report. www.peer.eu, accessed 3 March 2019.

2 Circularity, sustainability and labour in the circular industrial economy

Circular economy and sustainability have the same vision of a society which balances economic, environmental and social needs, based on a caring attitude. Economy and ecology go hand in hand because waste prevention is also a prevention of economic and resource losses. By extending the service life of goods through reuse, repair, remanufacture and technological and fashion upgrading, the circular economy substitutes labour-intensive service activities for energy and material intensive manufacturing activities.

2.1 The shift to a modern circular industrial economy

In the eighteenth century, the industrial revolution driven by the iron and coal industry enabled society to break free from the limits of natural resources and overcome the scarcity of food, goods, shelter, energy and infrastructure, ending a circular society of scarcity as old as mankind; steam engines and later electric motors freed mankind from the limitations of animal and human labour. Industrialisation turned this circular society into a monetarised industrial economy; time increasingly mattered, taxes on labour were introduced and concepts of liability for manufactured goods emerged.

In the late nineteenth century, the discovery of oil opened the road to the use of combustion engines, and in the mid-twentieth century to a multitude of synthetic fibres and man-made materials. 'Plastics' slowly replaced wood and metals in manufacturing. The fact that these new materials do not exist in nature, and that nature's circularity therefore could not 'digest' them, was of no concern.

In the short timespan between 1950 and today, industrial man filled space, the room around Earth within its gravity field, with millions of manufactured objects, and the oceans with an unimaginable amount of plastic objects, without any consideration of circularity, how to regain these objects at the end of their useful life.

In the late twentieth century, this *problematique* was amplified by a growing complexity of materials and industrial processes. Custom-made metal alloys have been increasingly used in producing many goods, just as rare earth elements: a smartphone today contains 70 elements of the 118 chemical elements of the periodic table, often in minute quantities. As end-of-pipe technologies do not allow recovering these atoms and molecules for reuse, most of the economic value of these material assets is lost after their first use (Material Economics 2018), despite general activities of recycling to recover material volumes.

Industrialised countries today have reached breaking point. After a long battle to overcome scarcities, the linear industrial economy has created a society of abundance with saturated markets for many goods; globalised production no longer increases wealth, but substitutes new for existing wealth. In addition, ever increasing waste volumes of synthetic materials and new material combinations push waste management costs ever higher. As these costs are borne by society at large, manufacturers have no economic incentive to control them.

The management of end-of-pipe waste is the final phase of the linear industrial economy, whereas waste prevention is one of the objectives of the circular industrial economy. At the point of sale, liability is transferred from the producer to the buyer-user (the consumer), who passes it on to the state. Consumer waste, as objects with no positive value or ultimate liable owner, become the liability of municipalities and nation states (Figure 2.1).

In a society of abundance, the circular industrial economy is nation states' solution of last resort to reduce waste. But emphasis is currently put on rapidly reducing the waste volumes (through recycling, incineration), not on maintaining the highest value and utility through reuse and service-life extension for

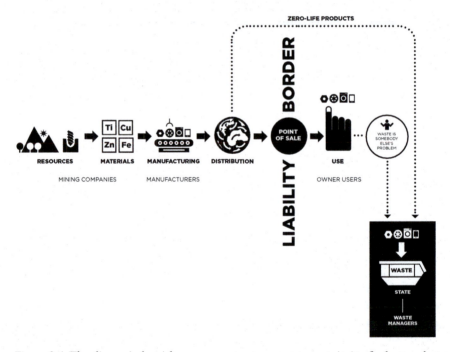

Figure 2.1 The linear industrial economy: waste management is its final step, but somebody else's liability

the longest period of time. The producers of the linear industrial economy are not involved in this process.

A modern circular industrial economy needs to emerge to overcome this legacy problem of a consumer society of abundance. This implies a triple shift:

- from the artisanal approach of a circular economy of necessity to the industrial approach of a circular industrial economy, both for manufactured objects and materials;
  - closed loops for objects to enable the reuse of goods and components at a quality as good as new (the era of 'R', see Chapter 4);
  - reversed material sciences to delink used materials in order to recover molecules and atoms for reuse at the same purity as virgin resources (the era of 'D', see Chapter 5);
- from the present producer liability for manufacturing quality to an Extended Producer Liability (EPL) also for end-of-service-life objects (closing the invisible liability loop, see Chapter 7);
- from a consumer attitude focused on fashion and newness of products to a user attitude focused on performance, function and sufficiency of solutions (achieving desired output from minimum input).

An intelligent management of stocks builds on 'sustainability' in the original meaning of the term, which comes from forestry and means maximising the interests from a stock or capital (forest) while conserving the capital itself.

2.2 Sustainability and the circular industrial economy

Sustainability has been at the heart of the circular industrial economy since it started. In 1713, Hans Carl von Carlowitz, responsible for the mining industry in Saxony (Sachsen), recognised the danger of a scarcity of timber for mining and metallurgy and concluded that only so many trees should be cut annually as could be regrown, maintaining the forest capital. He called this industrial resource policy *Nachhaltigkeit*, 'sustainability' (Carlowitz 1713).

Prussian Junkers, landowner-foresters, then adopted the term 'sustainable forestry' to define their maxim of optimising the interests from their forests (animals, fruit, plants, topsoil) while maintaining and improving both quantity and quality of the stock (the forest and its trees, but also the water retention capacity of the soil). They were capitalists caring for nature because the forests – nature – were their main source of income and wealth.

Caring thus has been the attitude at the roots of sustainability and circular economy right from the beginning.

Caring implies a personal relationship, often over a long period of time, with a stock of goods (forests, animals), a person (in medicine or friendship) or an object (*Zen and the art of motorcycle maintenance*, Pirsig 1974); examples are natural parks, objects in museums and UNESCO World Heritage sites. By contrast, the term caring is absent in the vocabulary of the linear industrial economy.

In the late twentieth century, sustainability was adopted as a political concept, first in the 1972 UN Conference on the Human Environment in Stockholm, which was followed by the 1992 UN Conference on Environment and Development in Rio. The Rio Declaration reaffirmed and built upon the Stockholm Declaration, systematising and restating existing normative expectations regarding the environment, as well as boldly positing the legal and political underpinnings of sustainable development in a document called Agenda 20.

In a beginner's way, sustainability and circular industrial economy can be regarded as two faces of a coin, as shown in Figure 2.2.

The key objective of a circular industrial economy is to keep the economic value and utility of stocks of manufactured objects and materials as high as possible for as long as possible. Use (or utilisation) value is the dividend we harvest without consuming the stocks themselves.[1]

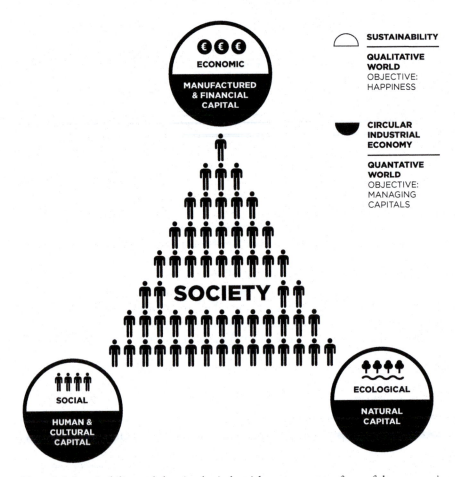

Figure 2.2 Sustainability and the circular industrial economy: two faces of the same coin

Wealth in the circular industrial economy is measured as the sum of the quality and quantity of all stocks; growth is an increase in the sum of the quality and quantity of all stocks, not an increased throughput. Statistics measuring national wealth in this sense have only just started to be published (World Bank Group 2018).

Now production optimisation has always included in-house loops of reuse and recycling in order to minimise costs. Clean production waste has thus been sold back to material producers for reuse, from the goldsmiths' famous table-pockets to plastic extruder process waste.

Robert Bosch, founder-owner of Bosch Company in Stuttgart, was known to pick up paper clips lying on office floors and tell employees 'not to waste my money':

> Economy and ecology meet in sustainable business models because waste prevention is also a prevention of economic and resource losses!

Preventing a catastrophic loss, such as a fire in a major building, not only prevents the environmental damages caused by the fire itself, but also those caused by the fire brigade in its effort to contain the fire. Take the explosion followed by a fire in a chemical warehouse in Schweizerhalle, near Basel, in 1986. The runoff of the water sprayed by the fire brigade on the burning warehouse, to prevent the fire from spreading to other buildings, polluted the Rhine River, killing all animal life downstream from Basel.

The insurance premiums to cover the Environmental Liability for buildings can be up to 100 times the premium to cover the value of the building itself. Many fire brigades now allow a building on fire to burn down completely, focusing their efforts on preventing the fire from spreading to other buildings nearby, to limit total damages.

Industrial Symbiosis and Industrial Ecology have extended the strategy of cost reduction through a cascading use of resource flows, such as waste heat. This strategy has been perfected in the Kalundborg eco-industrial park, reducing both cost and preventing waste in industrial production that is before the point of sale (Chapter 6). But these strategies have no impact on the use phase of manufactured objects after the point of sale or on end-of-pipe waste issues, and thus greatly differ from the reuse and service-life extension loops of the circular industrial economy. In addition, they do not allow exploiting the opportunities of the Performance Economy, such as selling goods as a service. And Industrial Symbioses contains a catastrophe risk management issue: the German Democratic Republic (DDR) was a near-perfect attempt of an Industrial Symbioses on a national level; this contributed to the rapid collapse of its economy after German unification in 1989, due to a complete lack of resilience and redundancy.

To summarise, the circular industrial economy:

• is sustainable because it maintains existing resource investments to fulfil market needs instead of relying on new material and energy resources;

- manages manufactured stocks (physical capital), such as forests, cities, fleets of vehicles and equipment, by balancing the use of human, manufactured, natural and financial assets;
- allows a decoupling of wealth and welfare creation from resource consumption and is best done locally, where its clients are;
- promotes service-life extension activities, which are part of a trend of intelligent decentralisation, like 3D print, AI-led robotised manufacturing, micro-breweries and bakeries as well as urban farming.

Where objects are expected to be lost into the environment, preference should be given to biodegradable materials, which nature's circularity can digest, or to alternative technical reuse solutions, such as 'propulsive rocket landing'. For example, the Falcon 9 rocket developed by Space X is the first reusable rocket, able to land on its launch pad after a mission and not turning into space waste or crashing into the sea.

2.3 Labour in the circular industrial economy

> In manufacturing, three quarters of energy is used in the production of basic materials such as cement and steel, only one quarter in producing goods such as buildings or cars: for labour input, the relation is reverse, three quarters being used in producing the goods.
>
> (Stahel and Reday-Mulvey 1976)

By extending the service life of goods through reuse, repair, remanufacture and technological and fashion upgrading, the circular industrial economy employs labour-intensive activities of a nature similar to producing goods, to the detriment of energy and material intensive ones of producing basic materials.

The circular industrial economy, replacing the production of new goods, thus substitutes manpower for energy, and local workshops for centralised factories, enabling local job creation and the reindustrialisation of regions. Taxes on labour versus taxes on resources become a key policy issue in the shift towards a circular industrial policy (Stahel 2013).

This is of importance because labour is of a special nature, unlike the other factors of production.

> Human capital is unique because it is not only a renewable resource—like trees—but also the only resource with a qualitative edge; its quality can be improved through education and training but will deteriorate rapidly if unused. People, human capital, are a key—but often forgotten or under-exploited—capital in any economy.
>
> (Stahel 2013)

Schumacher had highlighted the role of labour in *Small is beautiful*, the original title of which was *Economics as if people mattered* (Schumacher 1973).

Innovation and human capital are Siamese twins; the sources of innovative ideas are therefore not limited to R&D centres and academia. Some manufacturers have successfully understood the innovation potential of their shop floor workers in HSE (Health, Safety and Environment) topics, such as DuPont de Nemours' Sustainability Awards, and the German Railways' *Vorschlagswesen*, motivating and rewarding workers for proposing improvements to their daily work activity and environment. Another approach to maintain the highest manufacturing quality is used in Toyota's car factories, where every employee who discovers a fault can stop the production line; the fault is then immediately corrected by experts rushing to the scene. When opening the original factory to produce the first generation of RAV4 vehicles, the president of Toyota explained the fact that only few robots were present in the factory with Toyota's quest for permanent improvements – which only workers were able to fulfil.

Learning by doing is also an integral part of the circular economy of craftsmen and of SMEs. Spreading this knowledge – technical and economic – to class- and boardrooms, to academia and technical training institutions, and to new 'R' professions is a major challenge in speeding up the transition to a circular industrial economy.

Note

1 A sustainable economy is based on asset management and focused on use; the term 'sustainable production and consumption' is an oxymoron for any manufactured products with the exception of food and feedstuff, and should be replaced by 'sustainable use'.

References

Carlowitz, Hans Carl von (1713) *Sylvicultura economica.*
Material Economics (2018) Ett värdebeständigt svenskt materialsystem (Retaining value in the Swedish materials system). Economic value measured in billion Swedish Kroner versus material measured in tonnes. Research study, unpublished.
Pirsig, Robert (1974) *Zen and the art of motorcycle maintenance.* William Morris and Company, London.
Schumacher, Fritz (1973) *Small is beautiful: Economics as if people mattered.* Harper & Collins, New York.
Stahel, Walter (2013) Policy for material efficiency: Sustainable taxation as a departure from the throwaway society. *Philosophical Transactions A of the Royal Society*, vol. 371, pp. 1–19.
Stahel, Walter R. and Reday-Mulvey, Genevieve (1976) The potential for substituting manpower for energy. Report to the Commission of the European Communities, Brussels. Published in 1981 as *Jobs for tomorrow, the potential for substituting manpower for energy.* Vantage Press, New York.
World Bank Group (2018) The changing wealth of nations report 2018. https://openknowledge.worldbank.org/bitstream/handle/10986/29001/9781464810466.pdf, accessed 15 January 2019.

3 The circular industrial economy, a wealth of new opportunities

The circular industrial economy manages the stocks of manufactured objects after the point of sale, which are controlled by the owner–users (called the era of 'R'), and the stocks of manufactured materials, controlled by economic actors recovering resources (called the era of 'D'). A mature circular industrial economy will integrate the two domains and the linear industrial economy into one single loop, with the use value replacing the exchange value as the central economic value. A shift to such a mature circular industrial economy would substantially reduce greenhouse gas (GHG) emissions and increase the number of jobs.

3.1 Shifting from a circular society to a circular industrial economy

Early man lived in a circular society of scarcity driven by necessity, which still exists in industrially less developed regions of the world. A circular economy manages stocks of assets with the objective of maintaining their value in both qualitative and quantitative terms for as long as possible in a monetarised world. Owner–users of objects and resources are in control in the circular society and economy (Figure 3.1).

Clashes between circular and linear systems are frequent, for example when indigenous people living in and from natural habitats – a high-value long-term capital or stock – are confronted with logging companies and geologists searching for oil or mineral deposits that can be rapidly industrially exploited. The latter will produce monetarised revenue only for a limited period of time, for these high-value producer-controlled flow processes will deplete the natural and cultural capital, destroying the (non-monetarised) stocks.

The circular economy is thus about maximising the use value of stocks within the vision of a sustainable society, encompassing stocks (assets, capitals) of natural, human (work and acquired skills), cultural (material and immaterial), financial and manufactured nature – objects and materials – through an economic lens. The latter is key as it focuses on economic value, which in turn introduces ownership and liability – notions which do not exist in the circularity of nature.

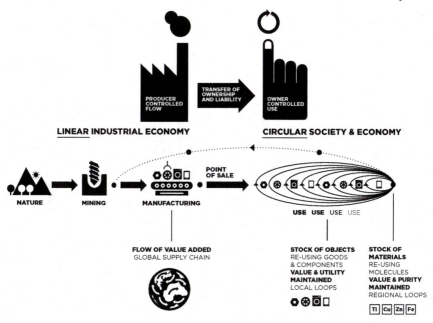

Figure 3.1 The characteristics of the linear industrial economy and the circular society and economy

The circular industrial economy focuses primarily on the stocks of manufactured objects after the point of sale controlled by the owner-user, and second on the stocks of manufactured materials. Today, the circular industrial economy is complementary to the linear industrial economy, which produces the objects that form the stocks of the circular industrial economy. In a mature circular industrial economy, production becomes an integrated part of it (Figure 3.3). Mining industries may feel left out in a circular industrial economy, yet could occupy the driver's seat if they shift to renting molecules in a Performance Economy (see Chapter 8) instead of selling materials.

In a 2018 report entitled 'From waste to resource productivity, evidence and case studies', the UK Government Chief Scientific Advisers state that: 'waste is actually an enormous opportunity. Much of it is a potential resource that can be recovered and reused in a huge number of ways' (UK OGL 2017).

3.2 Analysing the circular industrial economy

The circular industrial economy manages stocks of manufactured objects with the objective to maintain their value and utility as high as possible for as long as possible; and stocks of molecules with the objective to maintain their highest purity and value for as long as possible. The probably first graphic presentation of the circular industrial economy dates from 1991 (Stahel 1991) and is reproduced schematically in Figure 3.2.

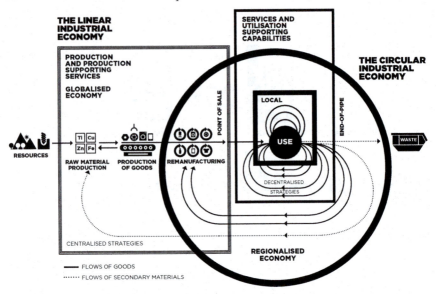

Figure 3.2 Situating the linear industrial economy, the circular industrial economy and the Performance Economy.

This early diagram already clearly distinguishes three key domains of the circular industrial economy:

- in the circle, the loops of managing the utilisation or use phase of stocks of manufactured objects and their components, by maintaining the value and quality of infrastructure, buildings, investment goods, equipment and durable consumer goods in a local or regional economy;
- in the small square, the local use-focused Performance Economy;
- the hatched line of flows of used materials returning to the raw material producer to recover molecules and atoms in a globalised economy.

The first two domains, focused on the utilisation phase of manufactured objects, open a number of new industrial opportunities and strategies, which are of less interest to the linear industrial economy as they are service activities, which are considered non-productive.[1]

The opportunities include for the:

- first domain: service-life extension of goods, through reuse, repair, remanufacture and technological upgrading of goods and components (in the following called era of 'R');
- second domain: long-life goods, multifunctional goods, and such systems solutions as selling goods as a service (rental, leasing), shared, common and multiple use, selling quality monitoring instead of replacement products (in the following called Performance Economy);

- third domain: recovery of molecules and atoms, in the 1991 report this domain was structured under recycling of clean production scrap, pure material 'end-of-pipe' waste and mixed end-of-pipe waste (in the following called era of 'D').

The shift from an artisanal local to an industrial regional circular economy started in the second half of the twentieth century with the remanufacture of one-off objects to 'as good as new' condition by Small and Medium Sized (SME) workshops, as a service for owners of the objects. Then independent service companies specialised in remanufacturing mass-produced equipment, such as automotive components and vending machines, appeared, followed by fleet managers – owner-users of large stocks of equipment, such as armed forces, railways and airlines – who developed their own maintenance, repair and remanufacture activities, including technologies, tools and methods to improve remanufacture and enable technological upgrading to 'better than new' quality.

In the last decade of the twentieth century, Original Equipment Manufacturers (OEM) of photocopiers (Xerox Corp.), truck engines (Caterpillar) and car engines and gearboxes (Volkswagen) pioneered remanufacture with technological upgrading as new industrial strategy, combined with buying back the broken and reselling the remanufactured objects (Caterpillar, Volkswagen), or by selling goods as a service (Xerox selling customer satisfaction).

In a mature circular industrial economy, the domains of objects and materials become integrated into one single loop, which also integrates the linear industrial economy supplying innovative new materials and components. Figure 3.3 shows this mature circular industrial economy by using a backcasting approach. 'Backcasting' is the opposite of forecasting; the observer defines the result that he wants to achieve, puts himself in this future position and then analyses opportunities and risks looking back. For ease of reading, links to the following chapters are added. Such a circular industrial economy has the potential to become the industrial default option of a sustainable society.

The macro-economic impact of such a mature circular industrial economy has been researched pertaining to the Czech Republic, Finland, France, the Netherlands, Poland, Spain and Sweden by Anders Wijkman and Kristian Skanberg. In their 2016 study, they have calculated that a nation-wide shift to a circular industrial economy would reduce greenhouse gas (GHG) emissions by 66 per cent and increase the number of jobs at national level by more than 4 per cent (Wijkman and Skanberg 2016). This reduction of 66 per cent is way above any figures discussed in the political agenda of slowing global warming, such as the COP 21 conference in Paris. Conference of Parties (COP) meetings are organised under the leadership of the UN with the aim to find political solutions to stop global warming. COP 24 took place in Katowice in December 2018.

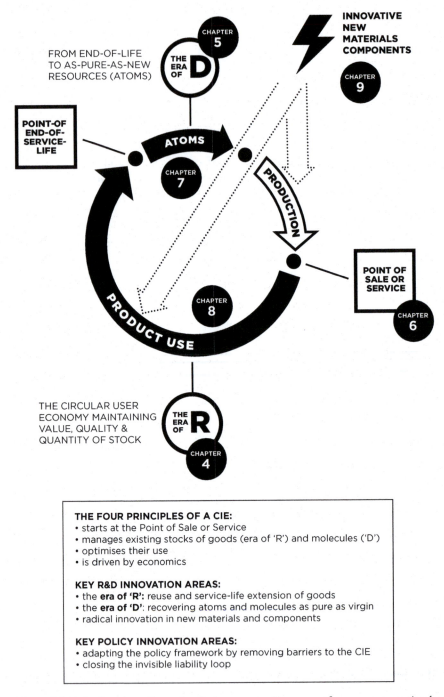

FROM END-OF-LIFE
TO AS-PURE-AS-NEW
RESOURCES (ATOMS)

INNOVATIVE
NEW
MATERIALS
COMPONENTS

CHAPTER
9

CHAPTER
5

THE
ERA
OF **D**

POINT-OF
END-OF-
SERVICE-
LIFE

ATOMS

CHAPTER
7

PRODUCTION

POINT OF
SALE OR
SERVICE

CHAPTER
6

PRODUCT USE

CHAPTER
8

THE CIRCULAR USER
ECONOMY MAINTAINING
VALUE, QUALITY &
QUANTITY OF STOCK

THE
ERA
OF **R**

CHAPTER
4

THE FOUR PRINCIPLES OF A CIE:
• starts at the Point of Sale or Service
• manages existing stocks of goods (era of 'R') and molecules ('D')
• optimises their use
• is driven by economics

KEY R&D INNOVATION AREAS:
• the **era of 'R'**: reuse and service-life extension of goods
• the **era of 'D'**: recovering atoms and molecules as pure as virgin
• radical innovation in new materials and components

KEY POLICY INNOVATION AREAS:
• adapting the policy framework by removing barriers to the CIE
• closing the invisible liability loop

Figure 3.3 A backcasting view of today's opportunities, seen from a mature circular industrial economy

A mature circular industrial economy is intertwined with the linear industrial economy in two ways, the latter serving to:

- upgrade existing stocks by introducing innovative materials and components; and
- replace stocks that have become technically or fashion-wise obsolete or have been destroyed.

In fact, the linear industrial economy becomes one of the segments of the big loop of a mature circular industrial economy.

3.3 Some principles underlying the circular industrial economy

The circular economy is a better economy because it uses resources more efficiently. Maintaining the value and utility of stocks for the longest period of time, the key feature that distinguishes the circular industrial economy from the linear industrial economy introduces the 'Factor Time' – no limits – into economics, ultimately also with regard to liability (see Figure 8.5).

By extending the service-life of objects and materials, the circular economy reduces the speed of resource flows through the economy and directly impacts the production volumes and end-of-pipe waste volumes of the linear industrial economy: in the saturated markets of industrialised countries, doubling the service life of goods halves both production and waste volumes.

Making the circular industrial economy the default option of a sustainable society will be facilitated by behavioural shifts, such as stewardship replacing ownership, and personal bottom-up motivation – Saint-Exupéry's longing for the sea – complementing top-down command-and-control legislation. Adapting policy frameworks to reflect the changed objectives of managing stocks instead of flows, and of maintaining the values of stocks instead of creating value added in production, may be the biggest challenge for governments and thus promises to become a driver of sustainable competitiveness between nations.

The separate silo-liabilities for take, make, sell, use, dispose and manage waste of the linear industrial economy will gradually have to give way to an overall stewardship and even liability for maintaining stocks at their highest value. A mature circular industrial economy will need a 'stewardship value' method to monitor changes in the quality and quantity of stocks over time, which is distinct from the 'supply chain management' method of the linear industrial economy, used to minimise production costs up to the point of sale. Supply chain management is the active management of supply chain activities from product development, sourcing, production and logistics to the point of sale, as well as the information systems needed to coordinate these activities.

3.4 Which external factors drive the circular industrial economy?

A number of external factors fuel the growth of the circular industrial economy. Urban regions may run out of landfill sites, for instance for construction waste, and favour the transformation of buildings instead of their demolition; or policymakers may push for lower dependency on resource imports or waste exports for political reasons, and as a result promote or legislate longer service-lives of objects. Individuals may develop increased attitudes of caring for objects for sentimental or status reasons – witness the rapidly growing number of vintage vehicles – or nations could emphasise the role of cultural heritage to maintain political stability.

The result will be increasing business volumes of reuse, repair and remanufacture, outpacing the capacity of local SMEs, enabling economies of scale and leading to regional circular industrial economies with more industrialised processes – witness the textile leasing sector – and to manufacturers entering the market for circular industrial economy services. These newcomers could learn from existing fleet managers, such as railways and airlines, which is also an obvious learning pool for business schools (Scott and Stahel 2013).

An emerging external factor is 'government liability' claims by groups of citizens, attacking the fact that governments are not taking actions to fulfil their promises made under the COP 21 agreement to limit global warming to 2°C in the near future. Activities of the circular industrial economy would qualify as CO_2 compensation measures to fight off these claims in court (see Chapter 10 for details).

3.5 The value fork

Within the circular industrial economy, there are differences in the tasks and values between the two key domains of maintaining the value and utility of stocks of manufactured objects (the era of 'R') and maintaining the value and quality (purity) of stocks of molecules and atoms (the era of 'D').

These differences need to be taken into account with regard to ownership and control. The era of 'R' is controlled by owner-users, both individuals and corporates; the era of 'D' is controlled by the economic actors in charge of end-of-service-life objects.

- The era of 'R' can appear as inhomogeneous because the stock of goods in use is geographically dispersed, of a high diversity and because 'R' activities reach from local ones for tailor-made objects, to the regional remanufacture of mass-produced goods.
- To enable the best value preservation of stocks of objects, owner-users in the era of 'R' should have the right to reuse and repair objects as long as they see fit. As the technical complexity of objects increases, this right is increasingly restrained by producers (OEMs), through such strategies as premature product obsolescence and technical incompatibility of new objects with existing stocks.
- The era of 'D' is a suitable case for material innovation and technology solutions to sort high-volume low-value end-of-service-life materials, commonly referred to as 'waste', and turn it into molecules 'as good as virgin'.
- To enable the best value preservation of stocks of molecules, owners of materials embodied in end-of-service-life objects should have a duty to

sort and de-link the materials in order to recover molecules of highest purity. In the case of fugitive materials, such as plastics in the oceans, objects could be commercialised through rent-a-molecule strategies instead of being sold, or producers forced to accept an Extended Producer Liability (EPL, see Chapter 6).

But at the end of a service-life of goods, who decides which of these two options should be given preference? And on which criteria should this decision be based?

The circular industrial economy is about economics; the overarching principle should therefore be economics! Environmental and social benefits will be a result, but only exceptionally the decision criteria.

A simple economic rule says that:

> The use value of a product is higher than the sum of the value of the materials it is made of.

The manufacturing principle of value added is living proof of this rule, as the market value per unit of weight increases from raw material to manufactured component to finished product. In a mature circular industrial economy, solutions in the era of 'R' should therefore be preferred over solutions in the era of 'D'. Product use optimisation is clearly more profitable for the product owner than selling the product for scrap to recover atoms and molecules (see Figure 5.2).

But the end of the service-life of objects falls into a control vacuum. The new owners of used objects – 'recyclers turned resource managers' – act under legal and time pressure and their knowledge and business contacts are mostly in the era of 'D', not 'R'. For mobile objects, the short-cuts of shredding, incineration and landfill are often the easy and quick way in waste management, but destroy the value and utility of stocks.

The disassembly of objects into components and clean fractions of materials, followed by their remarketing, is labour and knowledge intensive and for many economic actors unknown territory, 'the road not taken' (Frost 1916).

This problem is even more acute for immobile objects, such as infrastructure and buildings. Buildings, which no longer serve a purpose or cannot be transformed or adapted for new uses, could at least partly be dismantled and their components reused, but time pressure is often the dominating factor in demolishing built structures. They are blown up or smashed to bits, and the resulting waste used at the lowest value, for instance in road construction.

Yet about 80 percent of the material and energy resources initially spent to build a structure are embodied in the load-bearing structure. These resources are preserved in the reuse and repair options of the era of 'R', but mostly lost in the era of 'D'.

Designing buildings as modular systems of standardised components, which can be reused after dismantling, is part of an emerging trend of designing building components for a multiple life in the era of 'R'. Considering infrastructure and constructions as material banks to confront potential problems of resource supply in the future is a new trend in the era of 'D'.

3.6 Innovation challenges in the circular industrial economy

These challenges are of a holistic nature and concern economic actors as much as policymakers.

The era of 'R' is the best known part of the circular industrial economy, but spreading the knowledge to boardrooms and classrooms, academia and professional training institutions and public procurement agencies is wanting.

The era of 'D' is a largely unexplored Research & Development domain, with no national borders. Many innovative solutions will be patentable and provide a long-term competitive advantage to its finders (Chapter 9).

Exploiting the potential of systems solution and the corresponding innovative techno-commercial business models of the Performance Economy is an opportunity ignored, or the changes of their implementation feared, by many corporate actors.

National policies to holistically exploit the social, ecologic and economic opportunities inherent in the circular industrial economy are rare, partly because policymaking is organised in silos, similarly to academia (scientific disciplines), macro-economy (industrial sectors) and micro-economy (departments in a company). But innovative sustainable solutions are mostly multidisciplinary and multi-sectoral – and need a new policy thinking outside the box.

China released a Circular Economy Promotion Law in 2008, which was enforced in 2009 (Stahel 2009; Zhu 2016). Since then, the Party Congress of the People's Republic of China sets new circular economy targets every year within its Five Year Plan during the annual Congress. By comparison, the EU Waste Directive of 2008, which had waste prevention through reuse and service-life extension as its priority strategy, was never transferred into national legislation by most EU Member States. The Framework Programme FP7 of the European Union, Horizon 2020, is also an effort to catch up.

In 2017, researchers at the Institute of Sustainable Development and Management at Tongji University in Shanghai, People's Republic of China, published a working model of sustainability science, consisting of three cycles: the circulation of wastes, the circulation of products, and the circulation of services, corresponding to the era of 'D', the era of 'R' and the Performance Economy in this book (Zhu *et al.* 2017). Today, the People's Republic of China may have become the leading country in pursuing the circular industrial economy on a scientific level.

Note

1 Productive labour, according to Adam Smith, was any work which fixed itself in a tangible object, which is (re)vendible.

References

Frost, David (1916) *Mountain interval*. Henry Holt, New York.

Scott, Jonathan T. and Stahel, Walter R. (2013) *The sustainable business workbook: Waste elimination*. Greenleaf Publishing, Sheffield.

Stahel, Walter R. (1991) *Waste minimization case studies for three products*. U.S. EPA, R&D Office, Washington, DC. Translated from the 1991 report 'Langlebigkeit und Materialrecycling' for the Ministry of the Environment Baden-Württemberg, Stuttgart.

Stahel, Walter R. (2009) Chinese translation of *The performance economy*, first edition 2006, published in Simplified Mandarin, translated by Dr Zhu Dajian.

UK OGL (2017) *From waste to resource productivity, evidence and case studies*. The UK Government Office for Science, London.

Wijkman, Anders and Skanberg, Kristian (2016) *The circular economy and benefits for society,, jobs and climate clear winners in an economy based on renewable energy and resource efficiency*. The Club of Rome, Winterthur. www.clubofrome.org/wp-content/uploads/2016/03/The-Circular-Economy-and-Benefits-for-Society.pdf, accessed 20 March 2019.

Zhu, Dajian (2016) Circular economy: a new economic model for China and the world. *Les cahiers du Comité Asie de l'Anaj-Ihedin*.

Zhu, Dajian, Han, Chuanfeng and Zhang, Chao (2017) A working model of sustainability science. *Nature*, vol. 544, no. 7651.

4 The era of 'R'

The owner decides locally

In the circular industrial economy, the decision takers are the individual object owners. Their motivation to maintain the value and utility of infrastructure, buildings, equipment, vehicles, goods and other manufactured objects and their components at the highest level through reuse, repair and remanufacture are central. The era of 'R' is modern, economically profitable, ecologically desirable and socially viable; remanufacture is its most advanced activity.

4.1 Managing stocks of physical objects

The centre of the circular economy is YOU, the owner-user of objects.

- If one of your belongings is broken and you have it repaired, or you no longer want one of your belongings and sell it to somebody else, then you participate in the circular economy.
- If you no longer want one of your belongings and give it to somebody else who needs it, you are part of the circular society.

No man is an island – YOU act in synergy with other individuals and economic actors. If you dispose of an object and buy a new one, YOU are waiving your circular opportunities.

Within the circular industrial economy, the era of 'R' (Figure 4.1) is more profitable and resource efficient than the era of 'D', detailed in Chapter 5, because:

> the use value of an object is higher for the owner than the sum of the value of its materials; 'reusing goods' by extending their service-life therefore is more profitable and ecologic than 'recovering molecules' (recycling materials): reusing glass bottles is more profitable and ecologic than recycling glass to produce new bottles.

Craftsmen repairing clothes and vehicles or plumbers unblocking toilets against payment, in their workshop or on site, are actors of a circular economy mandated by the owner-user of the objects, as are workshops, which maintain fleets

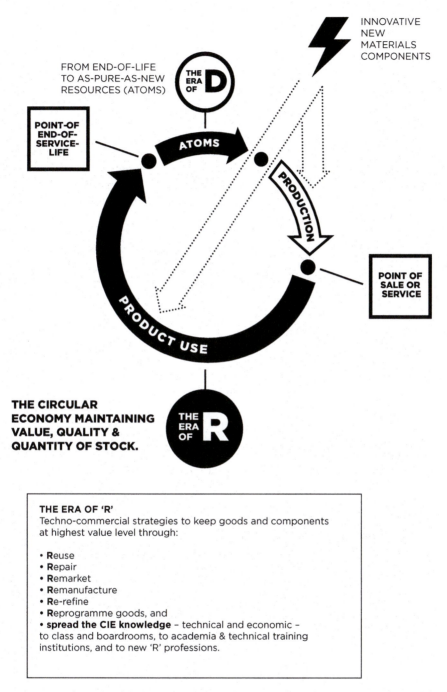

INNOVATIVE
NEW
MATERIALS
COMPONENTS

FROM END-OF-LIFE
TO AS-PURE-AS-NEW
RESOURCES (ATOMS)

THE
ERA
OF **D**

POINT-OF
END-OF-
SERVICE-
LIFE

ATOMS

PRODUCTION

PRODUCT USE

POINT OF
SALE OR
SERVICE

THE CIRCULAR
ECONOMY MAINTAINING
VALUE, QUALITY &
QUANTITY OF STOCK.

THE
ERA
OF **R**

THE ERA OF 'R'
Techno-commercial strategies to keep goods and components
at highest value level through:

• **R**euse
• **R**epair
• **R**emarket
• **R**emanufacture
• **R**e-refine
• **R**eprogramme goods, and
• **spread the CIE knowledge** – technical and economic –
to class and boardrooms, to academia & technical training
institutions, and to new 'R' professions.

Figure 4.1 The era of 'R', optimising product use through reuse and service-life
extension of goods and components

of equipment, such as shipyards repairing marine diesel engines or remastering entire vessels.

In these cases, the customers are owner–users of goods, individuals or companies motivated by care for their property, attracted by its patina or history and wanting to extend its service-life.

Other people may exchange objects or give them away for reuse, and repair clothes or vehicles for free to help neighbours, acting in a non-monetary circular society of self-help and charity outside the economy.

All these actions enable individuals and companies to enjoy the continued use of existing objects. The cooperation of owner–users and skilled workers enables optimising the use of objects and maintaining existing wealth and local jobs, minimising the consumption of material and energy resources.

The era of 'R' of the circular industrial economy can appear to economists at first as uneconomical because the stock of goods in use is geographically dispersed, of a high diversity and the activities of a service nature. This means there is little scope to introduce economies of scale to increase productivity. But these disadvantages are more than offset by the economic gains due to a minimal need for material and energy resources, which is inherent in the activities of the era of 'R'.

4.2 The decision makers

In the era of 'R', owners decide how and for how long they will use objects. Manufacturers and service SMEs compete for 'R' solutions to extend the service-life of objects.

For mobile goods, the era of 'R' is split into two distinct markets:

- individuals depending on local SMEs for repair services to extend the service-life of objects. Producers rarely offer take-back options, such as 'standard exchange' for small broken goods (tablets, smartphones), after the guarantee period,
- corporate owners (fleet managers) having themselves the knowledge and know-how to extend the service-life of the objects they own. Producers may provide periodic repair and maintenance services for sold objects, or function guarantees, as part of the sales contract.

For infrastructure and buildings, numerous SMEs provide local repair and maintenance services, while producers and major service companies offer longer-term maintenance service contracts for critical components, such as lifts. Producers may also sell goods as a service, such as offices and apartments for rent or lease.

But the decision takers are the objects' owners; their motivation to extend the service-life of goods, or to sell goods for reuse, is central. Creating individuals' desire to do so is one option to making the circular industrial economy society's default option; providing incentives to corporate owners to extend the service-life of goods, or to sell goods for reuse, could be a key strategy for policymakers (see Chapter 7).

4.3 The characteristics of the era of 'R'

The era of 'R' aims to maintain infrastructure, buildings, equipment, vehicles, goods and other manufactured objects and their components at the highest utility and use value at all times (OECD 1982). Maximising the use value of manufactured stocks over time and space follows some rules:

- the circular industrial economy is about economics but is counter-intuitive to manufacturing economics – small and local is now beautiful and profitable, instead of bigger and global being more profitable;
- the smaller the loops are – with regard to what is done and where – the more profitable and resource efficient they are; the inertia principle (Stahel 2010): *do not repair what is not broken, do not remanufacture something that can be repaired, do not recycle a product that can be remanufactured*;
- the lower the speed of the loops is, the more resource efficient they are, because of the law of reverse compound interests[1] and the second law of thermodynamics – each transformation step needs energy and loses part of the material;
- loops have no beginning and no end – newcomers can enter a loop at any point;
- the circular industrial economy substitutes manpower for energy and resources by managing manufactured stocks, whereas the linear industrial economy substitutes energy (machines) for manpower and manages production flows.

The era of 'R' is sustainable because:

- Part of a general twenty-first-century trend of intelligent decentralisation,[2] which embraces production and use: 3D printing (to produce cheap spare parts just in time), local production (micro-breweries, -bakeries, hydroelectricity, solar photovoltaic power), robot manufacturing, urban farming, soda fountains in pubs and at home; they are all local, decentralised, as are services of the era of 'R'.
- Economically profitable because 'R' activities for mass-produced goods are on average 40 per cent cheaper than equivalent newly manufactured objects with which they compete; this ratio is even higher when the differences of external costs with production are taken into consideration: 'R' activities are not subject to compliance costs (as there are no virgin resources from mining activities involved, there is no need to prove the absence of child labour, conflict minerals), nor carbon taxes or import duties and have a lower environmental impairment liability.

'R' business models differ from those of the linear industrial economy. The profitability of the former can be substantially higher than of single-use objects; witness the reusable rockets developed by the start-up companies Blue Horizon and Space X.

- Ecologically desirable because 'R' activities preserve most embodied resources (energy, material and water); they consume only few resources and cause little waste. As they are local, they do not need transport over large distances with intermediate storage, nor shopping centres and flashy packaging.

Steinhilper estimated the potential worldwide energy savings through remanufacture in 1997 to be the equivalent of the petrol in 350 crude oil carriers and the electricity produced by eight nuclear plants (Steinhilper 1998). The scarcity of data on this topic shows that this type of analysis does not yet interest mainstream economic research.

'R' activities do not depend on global publicity; they are invisible and silent, in contrast to linear industrial economy. Innovative ways of reaching the objects' owners through branding or marketing will gain importance in the shift from a circular economy to a circular industrial economy.

- Socially viable because 'R' activities are labour-intensive services best done locally where the clients are; they demand skilled labour to judge the minimal interventions necessary (the inertia principle); they partly rely on 'silver workers' with the skills and knowledge of technologies and objects of times gone by; and they nurture a caring attitude towards goods by owners and users.

'R' activities are labour and skill intensive because each step involves caring. Beginning with the non-destructive collection and value-preserving dismantling of used goods to analysing the repair or remanufacture options of each dismantled component demands a qualitative judgement. Developing innovative affordable repair and remanufacture methods for components traditionally destined for scrap is the ultimate engineering challenge in maximising profits in remanufacture.

The remanufacture of complex technical systems, combined with technologic and fashion upgrading can explain how environmental benefits and substantial savings in capital spending are possible: In 2005, the 59 ICE1 high speed trains of the German Railways were remanufactured at a cost of €3 million each, versus €25 million for a similar new train. The trains had covered 15 million km each in 15 years of service. This 'redesign' preserved 80 per cent of the initial resources of 16,500 tons of steel and 1,180 tons of copper per train; this corresponds to a prevention of 35,000 tons of CO_2 emissions and 500,000 tons of mining waste. The redesign included a technological upgrading of the rolling stock and a complete interior redesign, which allowed increasing the number of seats and thus the trains' profitability.

A big volume opportunity for 'R' activities is construction. In buildings, about a quarter of the labour input but 80 per cent of the resources consumed to build a structure are stored in its load-bearing structure, the reminder in fixings and equipment. Refurbishing buildings (changing fixings and equipment) saves the majority of resources embodied in the structure but may need as much labour as the initial construction (see the case study on the French construction industry in Stahel and Reday-Mulvey 1976).

Many buildings are also part of the cultural assets, of the national heritage; changes in use over time will necessitate conversions and innovative design solutions. One Wall Street is a 50-storey Art-Deco-style edifice in New York City, located in Manhattan's Financial District. It is a limestone spire with landmark protection on the corner of Wall Street and Broadway. Until 30 September 2015, it served as the global headquarters of the Bank of New York Mellon Corporation. Then Macklowe Properties bought it and is now redeveloping it into a 566-apartment building. To avoid the awkward layouts that can result from office conversions, and to create more apartments with windows, the elevators are displaced from a perimeter wall into the center of the building.

The construction industry, which is responsible for consuming about a third of all material resources, is an ideal case for remanufacturing, as the average life of a typical building is about 50 years. Remanufacturing the windows of old buildings enables the upgrade of the entire building to modern energy insulation standards, as was demonstrated at the Empire State Building, where in 2010 all 6,514 original windows were remanufactured on site to 'super-window quality' by the Rocky Mountain Institute (Ellen MacArthur Foundation 2016).[3]

Designing buildings as modular systems of standardised components, which can be reused after dismantling, could have a substantial impact on national resource consumption. The first commercial buildings designed following this principle have already been constructed in the Netherlands, such as an ABN (Allgemeene Bank of the Netherlands) building by the Dutch architect Thomas Rau.

Reversible building design or designing building components for a multiple life is also rapidly developing into a new domain of research both for architects' offices and universities (Durmisevic 2018). As part of the Global Research Challenge of ARUP London, the University of South Australia in October 2017 received funding for a project 'reuse of building components enabled by RFID, BIM, Internet and PSS' (Ness 2019). The Swiss Federal Institute of Technology (ETH) in Zurich is running its project, NEST, of a building, of which all components and equipment can be reused (NEST project at the ETH Zürich, www.empa.ch/web/nest).

4.4 Trust, skills and people, economic value and savings in the era of 'R'

Individual skills and value perception maximise economic profits in the circular economy – the real value is in the eye of the beholder: 'Antique dealers buy junk and sell antiques.'

The era of 'R' of the circular industrial economy creates novel jobs in new professions (Perutz and Stahel 1979, 1980). Restoring a vintage vehicle, an antique piece of furniture, an old painting or repairing an old clock or watch needs special tools and old skills, which today are only taught in few schools. New professions emerge, such as 'vehicle restorers' for the remanufacturing of oldtimer cars, which represent 3 to 5 per cent of the stock of automobiles.[4] In order to restore an oldtimer in an economically efficient way, vehicle restorers must master skills ranging from upholstery to remanufacturing different types of carburettors. Oldtimer cars increase in value over time, whereas any new car depreciates in value every year, and they enjoy certain privileges, such as entering 'environmental zones' in towns.

Hands-on vocational training is facilitated by repairing broken goods because (with the exception of heritage objects) it is based on zero-value objects. If a trainee 'destroys' an end-of-service-life object, experience is gained and only his labour input lost.

Economic considerations are decisive for most owners; developing innovative repair and remanufacture methods for components destined for scrap is the ultimate engineering challenge to increase the attractiveness of 'R' activities by reducing costs and maximising profits.

The economic feasibility of 'R' activities profits from the '*pars pro toto*' syndrome:

> In most repair situations, only few vital components are worn out or broken, such as the rubber joint of a fridge, or the engine of a vehicle. Repairing or remanufacturing this component allows maintaining the value of the whole object—the part saves the whole, 'pars pro toto'.

This phenomenon is especially pronounced for custom-made complex vehicles, such as ambulances, fire engines, aircraft – 'Airforce One' is 30 years old – as well as immobile objects such as infrastructure, power stations, buildings, which are components of larger systems.

Limitations in time and space can be overcome by away-grading (Stahel 1982): remarketing objects that have no more utilisation value in one location is possible by moving them to a different geographical region – mechanical typewriters still find buyers in areas without electricity – and by observing changing markets: for written communications of absolute confidentiality, mechanical typewriters are in great demand because they cannot fall victim to hackers. Many markets of the circular industrial economy have a niche character and high prices because of little competition.

Today, era of 'R' knowledge exists in SMEs and with fleet managers who are champions of reuse, repair and remanufacture for egoistic economic reasons, but is lacking in academia, public procurement agencies and the manufacturing industry. The biggest challenge to policymakers may thus be to spread the circular industrial economy knowledge – technical and economic – to class- and boardrooms, to academia and technical training institutions, and to public procurement agencies. In Europe, the European Circular Economy Stakeholder

Platform has picked up this challenge.[5] For the circular industrial economy needs managers and workers with a holistic understanding of systems whereas the linear industrial economy relies on specialised 'silo' education.

4.5 Putting flesh to the bones of the era of 'R'

The era of 'R' activities are of a great diversity; they may or may not involve a change of ownership, and transaction costs vary greatly. Some manufacturers of ballpoint pens, outdoor clothing, luggage (Eastpak), lighters (Zippo), give a life-long warranty; their distributors will repair broken goods free of charge. Some fleet managers mothball unused objects for future use (US Navy battleships) or as a supply of cheap spare parts (aircraft).

Reuse 'as is', resale and repurposing are profitable, ecologic and omnipresent

- Banknotes and coins have been exchanged between people for centuries; individuals and economic actors trade at second-hand markets and virtual marketplaces like eBay.
- Reuse in the building industry is common for temporary buildings, using modular building systems or inflatable structures, from the Bailey bridges of the Second World War to modern buildings made up of stacked pre-fabricated containers.
- Fleet managers have developed resale offices for objects and materials which are no longer needed, ranging from buildings and plots of land to surplus stocks of spare parts and used vehicles. 'DB Resale', for instance, is selling for reuse any object or material no longer needed or having become obsolete, owned by DB, the German Railways.
- The buy-back of used products by OEMs and distributors for clean-up and resale is increasingly popular, witness furniture manufacturers like USM and IKEA,[6] chair manufacturers in the United States and Europe, and garments from textile companies in the UK.
- Companies like rent-a-wreck buy used cars and successfully exploit them with minimal maintenance as cheap but profitable rental cars.
- Repurposing and conversion projects range from Russia's disused oil drilling platform transformed into the 'Sea Launch' rocket launch pad to airlines converting passenger planes, which are no longer popular with customers, into cargo planes, at a fractional cost of new cargo planes.
- Converting built structures is widespread, ranging from Barcelona's Olympic stadium of 1912 reused for the 1992 Olympics, and its bullring arena converted into a shopping centre, to Second World War fortifications in the Swiss Alps transformed into modern data storage facilities.

Repair activities are knowledge-intensive, often also of materials and technologies of the past, and enable maintaining human as well as manufactured capital:

- around 1720, Pierre Fauchard in Paris suggested that repairing teeth made better sense than pulling them out. As a result, Paris became the world centre of dental sciences for decades;
- numerous local SMEs offer commercial repair services for garments, vehicles, tyres, electronics and most mechanical and electro-mechanical equipment. Many of these services are better developed in industrially less developed regions than in countries with saturated markets;
- Patagonia operates mobile repair workshops, which travel to skiing or mountaineering events and repair outdoor clothing for free.

Remanufacture is the Rolls-Royce of the era of 'R', but its significance is difficult to grasp because of the large variety of activities. Twenty years ago, Professor Lund already found that remanufacturing operations are labour-intensive, critically dependent on a supply of labour and a reliable supply of good cores (used objects) at reasonable cost (Lund 1996). In 2016, the ERN started promoting remanufacture in Europe.[7] In 2018, a report by the International Resource Panel has reached similar conclusions as Lund 20 years earlier (IRP 2018) – what is needed to convince manufacturers of the linear industrial economy to change? The NASA space shuttle programme proved that remanufacture enables upgrading spearhead technology solutions over a period of 30 years. The champions of innovative remanufacture are fleet managers, such as armed forces, railways, airlines and facility managers, albeit only known to insiders:

- Remanufacture of custom-made objects is economically vastly superior to 'new', in addition to saving most of the resources that went into manufacturing. Fire engines, ambulances, lighthouses, cruise ships, aircraft and trains are typical examples.
- Remanufacture of mass-produced objects submitted to wear and tear, such as combustion engines, gearboxes and end-of-lease IT hardware allows a regular flow of used goods, economies of scale and cost savings of about 40 per cent compared to equivalent new goods. Smith and Keolian (2004) found that remanufacturing automotive engines lowered material consumption, GHG emissions and waste by 50 to 85 per cent, compared to manufacturing new engines.
- The quality of remanufactured objects can be 'better than new' for a number of reasons, such as material improvements through metallurgy factors inherent in use (engine block stability) or superior process technology (rail grinding has a tolerance ten times smaller than steel mill processes). In other cases, remanufacture is a necessary condition to maintain the use quality of objects which are part of our cultural assets, for instance the sound of Stradivari instruments.
- Speed can be a vital advantage of remanufacture: most battleships sunk in the attack on Pearl Harbor were re-floated, remanufactured on-site and recommissioned within a year of the attack.

Re-refining and *regenerating*: catalytic goods such as lubrication oils and solvents can be returned to their original quality, with reductions of CO_2 emissions ranging between 50 and 95 per cent, compared to virgin resources, according to a Study for the European Solvent Recycler Group, 'Carbon footprints of recycled solvents, comparison of CO_2 emissions between virgin and regenerated solvents'.

Re-programming: microchips designed to be reprogrammed enable upgrading instead of replacing IT hardware, online or in shops, preserving strategic resources and preventing waste.

Technologic and systems upgrading: replacing outdated components enables a rapid upgrading of existing objects to state-of-the art technology with minimal energy and material input and little waste. By adding new or replacing existing components, stocks of objects receive new use qualities:

- buildings are among the biggest energy consumers, for heating in cold and for cooling in hot climates. By improving the insulation capacity of their envelope (roofs, façades and cellars), many existing buildings can be upgraded to lower heating needs without touching the structure; adding façade elements to provide shade can reduce the need for cooling;
- micro-motors and latest technology batteries turn mechanical into electric bicycles;
- new mirrors and lights allow to 'produce' state-of-the-art lighthouses, without changing the lighthouse structure. Using 'coldzymes' instead of enzymes saves 80 per cent of the energy used by 'old' washing machines (traditional clothes washing machines use 90 per cent of the energy to heat water; enzymes collected from the Alps and Antarctica work in cold water and enable to produce 'cold-wash' enzymes);
- converting diesel engines to Compressed Natural Gas (CNG) reduces by one third CO_2, and almost completely NO_x and fine particle emissions.

Fashion upgrading: allows modernising the look of objects (textiles, cars) and facilitates high-price remarketing.

4.6 Research, innovation and policy challenges in the era of 'R'

Financial research is urgently needed to unearth the competitive advantages of 'R' activities, which today are only known to insiders. For example, the Return on Investment (ROI) of a remanufacturing plant is five times the ROI of a plant manufacturing the same objects, such as diesel engines. Convincing corporate CFOs and outside investors needs sound financial analysis.

From a technology point of view, the era of 'R' is a well-researched domain of the circular industrial economy, but implementation of the research results is lacking. Spreading this knowledge to academia and vocational training institutions as well as other industrial sectors should be a priority for policymakers. In Europe, perhaps, an Erasmus programme for manual skills, similar to the old

Hamburger companion system for carpenters, could help spreading the 'R' knowledge to more SMEs?

Spreading the acquired knowledge is also true for social learning. Remanufacturers learnt that buying back broken diesel engines at a price which depended on the condition of the broken engine – smashed up or not, and complete with all aggregates or not – created an attitude of caring in customers, lowered the cost and increased the profitability of the remanufacturing process. Treating end-of-service-life goods as broken or unwanted goods and not as waste makes a big difference with regard to environmental, social and economic sustainability of remanufacturing.

Research into user behaviour could also speed up the transformation. Building managers know that closing shutters and windows during certain times of the day considerably lowers a building's energy consumption. But the people living inside the buildings may have different priorities, such as direct light and natural ventilation.

Characteristics such as component standardisation and the material identity of objects may take on a new strategic importance in the future as they will have an influence on the value preserved, and therefore the profits of investors.

Notes

1   Reverse compound principle: a recovery process with an efficiency of 50 per cent conserves 50 per cent of material stock; this means that 50 per cent of the material is preserved in the first loop, 25 per cent in the second and only 12.5 per cent in the third.
2   A term first used by Professor Heinrich Wohlmeyer in Austria.
3   The remanufacture of the Empire State Building was designed and executed by the Rocky Mountain Institute, and quoted in *A new dynamic 2: Effective systems in a circular economy.*
4   Cars which are more than 30 years old (manufactured before 1988) are called old-timers and considered to be part of the technical heritage of a nation (EU Oldtimer Directive 20 May 2018). Their number is increasing every year, but the skills to maintain their technology and interiors are unknown for many young car experts.
5   A platform to exchange and interact, to make the change to a circular economy happen faster to the benefit of all. https://circulareconomy.europa.eu/platform/en, accessed 20 March 2019.
6   Second Life in Switzerland. In 2017, IKEA Spreitenbach tested a 'buy-back and resell service' (called second life service). The test was successful and as of 1 September 2018, all nine IKEA Switzerland stores will offer this service intended to extend the life of furniture and help conserve resources. Customers can check online whether their unused furniture meets the criteria for the buy-back programme and then take it to the store. The range includes more than 1,000 of the most popular products. IKEA buys the furniture back for up to 60 per cent of the original retail price, paying customers with IKEA vouchers. The furniture is then sold to other customers in IKEA's As-Is areas.
7   The European Remanufacturing Network (ERN), a pan-European project to understand the shape of remanufacturing in the EU. www.remanufacturing.eu/, accessed 16 January 2019.

References

Durmisevic, Elma (2018) Reversible building design. In Martin Charter (ed.) *Designing for the circular economy*. Routledge, London.

Ellen MacArthur Foundation (2016) *A new dynamic 2: Effective systems in a circular economy*. Ellen MacArthur Foundation Publishing, Cowes.

IRP (2018) Re-defining value – the manufacturing revolution. Remanufacturing, refurbishment, repair and direct reuse in the circular economy. www.resourcepanel. org/reports, accessed 26 December 2018.

Lund, Robert T. (1996) *The remanufacturing industry: hidden giant*. Boston University.

Ness, David (2019) *The impact of overbuilding on people and the planet*. Cambridge Scholars Publishing, Newcastle upon Tyne.

OECD (1982) *Product durability and product life extension, their contribution to solid waste management*. OECD, Paris.

Perutz, Peter and Stahel, Walter R. (1979) Vier Wege zu neuen Arbeitsplätzen (Four paths to new jobs). *Management Journal*, vol. 48, no. 2, pp. 81–85.

Perutz, Peter and Stahel, Walter R. (1980) *Arbeitslosigkeit – Beschäftigung – Beruf, Systembegrenzung und Lebensgestaltung (Unemployment – Occupation – Profession)*. Beiträge des Institutes für Zukunftsforschung Berlin, no. 11: Preisträgerarbeiten des GZ-Wettbewerbes 1977. Minerva Publikationen, Munich.

Smith, V.M. and Keolian, G.A. (2004) The value of remanufactured engines, lifecycle environmental and economic perspectives. *Journal of Industrial Ecology*, vol. 8, no. 1–2, pp. 193–222.

Stahel, Walter R. (1982) *The product-life factor*. http://product-life.org/en/major-publications/the-product-life-factor, accessed 20 December 2018.

Stahel, Walter (2010) *The performance economy*. Palgrave Macmillan, Houndmills.

Stahel, Walter and Reday-Mulvey, Geneviève (1976) The potential for substituting manpower for energy. Report to the Commission of the European Communities, Brussels.

Steinhilper, Rolf (1998) *Remanufacturing: The ultimate form of recycling*. Fraunhofer IRB Verlag, Stuttgart.

5 The era of 'D'

Economic actors recovering resource assets decide

The era of 'D' manages stocks of atoms and molecules – chemical elements – with the objective of maintaining the highest value and purity of these stocks. This implies a cultural change in waste management, from volume reduction to value capture, and a non-destructive collection of used goods and unmixed collection of used materials, which increases the profitability of the resource-cum-waste manager. Science is needed to develop innovative separating technologies.

5.1 Managing stocks of atoms and molecules

The centre of the circular economy is YOU, the owner-manager of used objects:

- If you dismantle used objects and re-market the components, which are only used but not broken, then you participate in the circular economy. The same is true if you sell the broken components to somebody else to recover the atoms and molecules.
- If you employ people who cannot work in the normal labour market to dismantle the used objects, you are part of the circular society.

Circularity in nature works well for natural materials, at nature's own pace. Where manufactured materials are dispersed in use (rubber wear from tyres, micro-plastics in sun creams) or deliberately disposed into the environment after use (drink containers), most manufactured objects and materials will cause a long-time environmental hazard, such as plastics in the oceans. Natural circularity can only de-bond natural materials, such as wood and wool, under favourable conditions and over time. It took a hundred years for nature to digest most of the materials which made up the *Titanic*, but the iron hull has survived to this day.

Market failures and a 'linear' approach to product design explain much of today's loss of value (of manufactured materials). The reasons for value losses are found throughout the value chain of multiple product categories, as well as the way in which current legislation is designed. Manufacturing

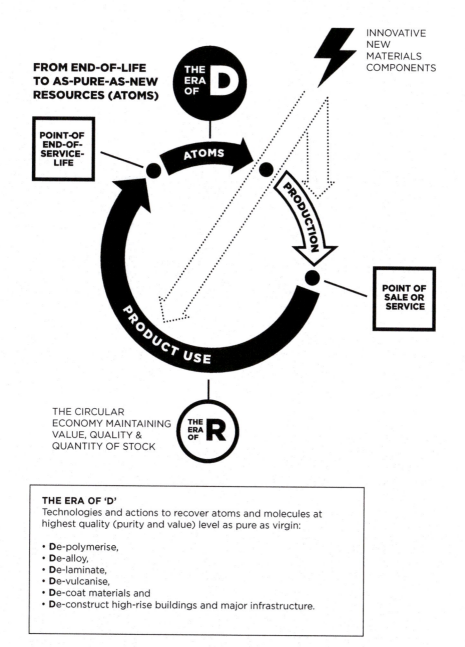

FROM END-OF-LIFE
TO AS-PURE-AS-NEW
RESOURCES (ATOMS)

THE ERA OF **D**

INNOVATIVE
NEW
MATERIALS
COMPONENTS

POINT-OF
END-OF-
SERVICE-
LIFE

ATOMS

PRODUCTION

POINT OF
SALE OR
SERVICE

PRODUCT USE

THE CIRCULAR
ECONOMY MAINTAINING
VALUE, QUALITY &
QUANTITY OF STOCK

THE ERA OF **R**

THE ERA OF 'D'
Technologies and actions to recover atoms and molecules at
highest quality (purity and value) level as pure as virgin:

• **De**-polymerise,
• **De**-alloy,
• **De**-laminate,
• **De**-vulcanise,
• **De**-coat materials and
• **De**-construct high-rise buildings and major infrastructure.

Figure 5.1 The era of 'D', recovering atoms and molecules – from end-of-life goods to
as-pure-as-new resources

companies have few incentives to design products so that materials can be recycled, notwithstanding policies such as 'extended producer responsibility'. Products therefore impose a negative externality on secondary materials production. Negative external effects also arise in the production of primary materials, but are rarely fully reflected in raw materials prices. Regulations and targets can also steer in the wrong direction, causing materials to be used as low-value aggregates.

(Material Economics 2018)

The era of 'D' of the industrial circular economy manages stocks of atoms and molecules with the objective of maintaining the quality (purity) and value of these stocks (Figure 5.1). But today, high-volume low-value recycling technologies are often seen as the solution of last resort in an 'out of sight out of mind' approach. This approach leads to the disposal of end-of-service-life objects – 'waste' – in order to minimise costs or due to a lack of appropriate recycling technologies. Maintaining the economic and resource value of the materials is not yet perceived as a priority. Yet extracting resources through mining costs money and creates environmental damages; waste prevention thus saves money and protects the environment. But policymakers and economic researchers focused on efficient production and economic growth disregard these opportunities because prevention activities slow GDP growth.

5.2 The need to identify decision takers to maintain highest value in the era of 'D'

At the 'end point of service-life', the decision for the highest value option depends on a mix of waste legislation and functioning markets between the owners of the used goods (waste/resource managers) and economic actors of the era of 'R' and the era of 'D'.

For individuals, the reuse or remarket option (era of 'R') involves substantial personal efforts under time, space, economic and sometimes legal pressure; the collect-and-dispose option, by contrast, can be easily delegated to municipalities in most urban areas.

Municipalities will use legal and cost criteria to make a choice between reuse, recycle and elimination options, such as landfill or incineration.

For 'waste' managers, the pursuit of maximum profit may be secondary to the need to minimise costs, or hindered by legal requirements, such as an obligation to destroy objects and recycle materials, even if they could achieve higher economic profits and lower environmental damage by remarketing used objects or components to the highest bidder (OEMs or era of 'R' actors). For example, in some regions, the use of disposable plastics instead of the sterilisation of durable objects may be imposed on hospitals by law in order to reduce the risk of pandemics.

The markets between used resource managers – owners of the used goods – and potential buyers of the era of 'R' will first need to be created; with few exceptions, they do not exist today: Vetrum, a Swiss company recovering glass bottles from bottle banks for sorting, quality inspection, sterilisation and reuse[1] and www.go4circle.be, [2] helping a wide body of companies to adopt circular economic principles, are the exception despite their high profitability, even in societies of abundance.

Three conditions have to be fulfilled for any activities of the era of 'D' to be effective (Figure 5.2):

- a safe transition from product use to the end point of service-life;
- a sorting into clean material fractions; and
- a continued ownership and liability for objects and embodied materials.

5.3 The characteristics of the era of 'D'

If and when manufactured objects or their components cannot be reused, the best option is to recover atoms and molecules at their highest utility and value (purity) for reuse (Figure 5.1). This demands technologies and processes to sort mixed (household) waste according to materials into clean fractions, and dismantle used objects into separate material fractions (for example different aluminium alloys) to enable the recovery of pure atoms and molecules (Müller 2018).

The era of 'D' is sustainable because:

- In economic terms, recovered molecules are in price competition with virgin resources. As commodity markets have a high price volatility, 'D'

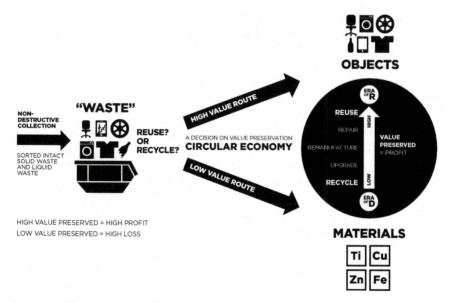

Figure 5.2 End-of-service-life business opportunities for value preservation: reuse or recycle?

materials with high collection costs are at a disadvantage. If manufacturers retain ownership of the material, this disadvantage shrinks because recovered molecules have lower transaction and compliance costs compared to virgin resources. Compliance costs arise in establishing certificates to prove the absence of child labour, conflict minerals and environmental impairment in virgin resources procured. In addition, recovered molecules pay no carbon taxes or import duties.

But in many cases, the technologies to recover molecules at a purity-as-new first have to be developed. These technologies will often differ from those used in the refining of virgin resources. 'Closing the high purity loop' will need considerable upfront investments in R&D (see Chapter 9).

- In environmental terms, recovering spent molecules – in comparison with producing virgin resources – prevents considerable volumes of mining waste and reduces the water and energy consumption of, and the negative impacts on the environment associated with, the mining and refining of virgin resources[3] (Schmidt-Bleek 1994).

Existing 'D' technologies are based on high volume global processes. If in the future the different alloys of a given metal are recovered separately, the volumes per fraction shrink and the transport distances between the locations of scrap collection and recovery process increase (Müller 2018).

A higher recovery quality will increase the economic value of the recovered molecules, but lead to a higher environmental impairment in the recovery process, if today's process technologies are used. A standardisation of metal alloys to reduce material diversity in production and the development of small volume 'mini-mills' would reduce transport distances and lower costs.

- In social terms, the main opportunities for skilled workers in the era of 'D' will be commercial – developing new markets between the owners of used goods (used resource managers), the buyers of the era of 'R' and the buyers of the era of 'D' – and in Research & Development to identify and develop innovative small volume process technologies to recover pure molecules. These research activities can be carried out on a global level wherever qualified labour and investment is available.

The labour input in the era of 'D' heavily depends on the value preservation choice of used objects, shown in Figure 5.2. The highest value preservation option necessitates labour-intensive non-destructive collection, dismantling and sorting processes, which have higher costs than collection by compactor trucks and demand higher efforts to remarket components and sorted scrap.

5.4 The foundation of the era of 'D': R&D, technology, knowledge and people

The three key opportunities are to:

- change attitudes from 'solution of last resort' in waste management to maintaining the highest value and purity of molecules;

- replace the concept of secondary resources in favour of a collection and recovery system of clean and sorted 'waste' fractions;
- create new and further develop current technologies and processes to recover pure molecular resources.

The export of mixed material wastes for recycling abroad, as part of the European waste management strategy of the last decades, is a thing of the past. China – the biggest recycler – in 2017 banned any imports of mixed materials for recycling, be it plastics or metals. Several other countries in Asia have followed China's policy.

This increases the pressure on governments, industry and academia in Europe to develop methods to recover pure high value atoms and molecules for reuse in manufacturing. Innovative industrial actors should be in the driver's seat of the era of 'D' because of the 'not invented here' syndrome. The Science and Technology opportunities to recover atoms and molecules are almost unlimited but only an early cooperation with industry will accelerate their application. Governments might ban the use of materials, which cannot be de-bonded, and promote new 'D' solutions and technologies that will emerge from research, such as to:

- de-polymerize plastics, currently done for nylon, fluorinated polymers (PTFE); or re-extrude plastic such as used HDPE;
- de-alloy metals; the presence of Ni, Cr or Cu in steel reduces the quality and economic value of steel; no technologies exist today to de-alloy these metals;
- de-laminate carbon-fibre composites, which are increasingly used in big volumes in the production of aircraft, automobiles and windmill blades; no technologies are used in Europe to de-link the composites and recover the molecules;
- de-vulcanize tyres to recover rubber and steel; several technologies exist but their commercialisation is hindered by subsidies to incinerate used tyres;
- de-coat objects; technologies to strip the paint off the fuselage of aircraft exist using CO_2 pellets or water jets in a closed loop instead of chemicals;
- de-construct high-rise buildings: an intelligent deconstruction of existing high-rise buildings allows actors to disassemble technical equipment and interior fittings for remarketing, and to recover part of the energy invested in the original construction; the higher the structure the more energy was needed to hoist materials up. This hoisting energy can be recovered when bringing the components and materials down in a smart deconstruction process, as was demonstrated in the deconstruction of a major hotel in Tokyo;
- de-construct major infrastructure: many infrastructures to produce electricity, such as dams and pressure pipelines, date from the early twentieth century and will be decommissioned in the coming decades. These are massive, sometimes monolithic constructions built to last and many will

have to be de-constructed at some point in the future. Off-shore wind-mills, with 75 per cent of total material input embodied in the underwater foundations, may be next.

However, there are limits to the era of 'D'. In some cases, such as nuclear power stations, the reuse of materials that have been irradiated may be illegal. In the case of dissipative uses, such as bituminous road surfaces containing broken glass to increase visibility at night and rubber from tyres to reduce tyre noise, it will be impossible to recover glass and rubber particles, but the bituminous mix as such can be re-melted and reused on-site.

5.5 The ownership fork

As many materials at the end of their service life have no or a negative value, the question arises who should do the activities of the era of 'D', and who should pay for it?

The recovery of pure atoms or molecules is feasible and established for few materials such as gold, silver and copper; where it is not, beginning-of-pipe preventive solutions, such as component design for multiple reuses, are environmentally more efficient than end-of-pipe resource recovery.

If prevention is impossible, profitable technologies can be developed for instance to recover pure phosphorous from municipal, and gold from industrial, waste water streams. Support for the era of 'D' may also come from research into single-atom technologies. The Centre for Single-Atom Electronics and Photonics, operated jointly by ETH Zurich and KIT Karlsruhe, has started looking at electronics and photonics.

Managers of used resources have a broad responsibility to achieve the main objective of the circular industrial economy, which is to maintain the highest value and utility for objects, and a stewardship to manage a material system that retains the highest value and purity of atoms and molecules. In order to achieve the highest return on their investments, they need the liberty to develop the solutions with the highest value preservation (see Figure 5.2). The use value of objects dwarfs their material value – in fact, many used goods have a negative economic value as recycling costs are higher than their scrap value. The non-destructive collection of such used objects as furniture and bottles, and end-of-life materials such as newspapers and plastics, and the sorting into pure material fractions is therefore a precondition to exploit the highest priced options. The higher the value preserved, the higher the waste manager's profit and incentive to prevent waste.

However, legislation may limit their liberty of action to maximise profits. The European Union's Directive on Waste of Electrical and Electronic Equipment (WEEE) may be a case in point. Introduced as a measure to extend the responsibility of manufacturers for end-of-service-life waste costs, the con-tractual obligations between manufacturers and waste managers may block the opportunities of the era of 'R' and oblige the latter to act exclusively in the era of 'D'. Policymakers are hindered by conflicting legislations, such as protecting the environment, Intellectual Property Rights, and the 'right to destroy' – which differentiates ownership from stewardship – in short, the lack of a holistic policy approach.

The unmixed collection of end-of-service-life materials creates an attitude of caring in customers and increases the profitability of the resource/waste manager. Treating used goods as broken goods, and used materials as unwanted materials – not as waste – makes a big difference with regard to environmental, social and economic sustainability of businesses. Topics such as product and component standardisation and the knowledge of the identity of all materials contained in objects take on a new strategic importance and can have a decisive influence on the value preserved, and therefore the profitability of the era of 'D' activities (see also Figure 5.2).

For manufactured objects and materials outside the circularity of nature, producers should accept liability for their products at the end of their service-life, because they had the choice of the:

- materials used in producing the objects and their components; using a limited number of standardised materials in product design and resource procurement would facilitate activities in the era of 'D' (Charter 2019);
- strategy to design goods in a systems approach, using standardised components for ease of disassembly, remanufacture and reuse;
- distribution channels, including the option of reverse logistics for later take-back or buy-back, in commercialising the objects.

5.6 Innovation and opportunities for policymakers in the era of 'D'

In the area of the built environment, recent policy interests in resource security and resource efficiency has fuelled research into the stock of materials embodied in existing infrastructure and constructions. Urban mining is one of the catch words used in this context (Baker-Brown 2018), but little information exists on the quality of these material deposits and suitability for later high purity recovery.

Buildings as Material Banks (BaMB)[4] aims to create ways to increase and sustain the value of building materials via a 'material passport', which lists all materials used in a construction by quantity and quality. Madaster Foundation,[5] designed as a public online library or archive of materials, components and products for reuse, pursues the idea that every building is a material depot. Registering the material input into new buildings should provide the basis for later urban mining activities (Oberhuber 2016).

In contrast to other manufactured objects, infrastructure and buildings can have service-lives of a hundred years or more. Only the future can tell if the quality of the embodied materials will satisfy the market's needs of the twenty-second century. Modular building systems using standardised components could probably greatly increase any options for a future reuse of building components or molecule recovery.

What is certain is that a circular industrial economy needs functioning markets to fulfil its objective of retaining the highest value and purity of objects and molecules. In this aspect, the circular economy does not differ from the linear industrial economy; it needs efficient marketplaces to remarket used goods and components as much as to recover pure molecules.

Notes

1 Vetrum: recovering glass bottles from bottle banks (collection points) for reuse. Vetrum AG is the leading Swiss company to sort, wash and test wine bottles: 7,000 bottles per hour, 16 million per year. More than 130 municipalities and organisations in eastern Switzerland send the wine bottles they collect from consumers to Vetrum for reuse. And more than two-thirds of the bottles received can be washed and remarketed for reuse. Turnover increased from 1.2 million bottles in 1992 to seven million bottles in 1998, and has tripled again since. Financial profit has doubled in the last five years. For one-third of the bottles, remarketing is not feasible and they are recycled (Stahel 2010, p. 237).
2 Go4Circle is the umbrella association for private Belgian companies who put the circular economy at the heart of their operations. It represents 220 companies who are helping enterprises across all sectors to fundamentally change their production processes, making the transition towards the circular economy. Between them, they employ around 8,000 people, accounting for an annual turnover of 2.8 billion euros.
3 Materials come with a multiple backpack of mining waste and environmental impairment. The backpacks of mining waste (measured in tonnes) differ for each material and are highest for rare metals such as gold (with a backpack of 500,000), lowest for plastics (with a backpack of 0.1). Manufactured capital in the form of infrastructure, buildings, goods and components has individual accumulated backpacks of all the materials and energies they embed, which have to be calculated individually.
4 Buildings as Material Banks (BAMB) is a research project under the EU Horizon 2020 Framework Programme.
5 Madaster is a private initiative by Thomas Rau and Sabine Oberhuber, which started in 2018 in the Netherlands.

References

Baker-Brown, Duncan (2019) Who is mining the Anthropocene? In Martin Charter (ed.) *Designing for the circular economy*. Routledge, London.

Charter, Martin (2019) *Designing for the circular economy*. Routledge, London.

Material Economics (2018) Ett värdebeständigt svenskt materialsystem (Retaining value in the Swedish materials system). Economic value measured in billion Swedish Kroner versus material measured in tonnes. Research study, unpublished.

Müller, Daniel (2018) Conference presentation at SINTEF Circular Economy conference, Trondheim, 31 May. Unpublished.

Oberhuber, Sabine (2016) *Material matters*. ECON im Ullstein Verlag, Berlin.

Schmidt-Bleek, Friedrich (1994) *Wieviel Umwelt braucht der Mensch? MIPS — Das Mass für ökologisches Wirtschaften*. Birkhäuser Verlag, Basel.

Stahel, Walter (2010) *The performance economy*, second edition. Palgrave Macmillan, Houndmills.

6 The point of sale, or factory gate, and liability

The regional circular economy begins at the point of sale, where the globalised linear industrial economy ends with a firework of marketing and publicity activities; the objectives of the two economies are worlds apart. Distributors and salesmen rule the point of sale, where ownership of, and liability for, objects change from the industrial producer to the individual buyer-owner or professional fleet manager. These two buyer groups differ fundamentally with regard to access to tools and knowledge of repair and maintenance, and their relationship with objects as 'tools' or 'toys'.

6.1 The point of sale as frontier between two economic philosophies

The centre of the circular economy is YOU, the salesman or distributor.

- If you give a life-long repair guarantee on the objects you sell, then you participate in the circular economy. The same is true if you offer free buy-back or take-back logistics and re-market returned objects or components, and if you provide access to information, affordable tools and spare parts to repair the objects in use.

The circular industrial economy is silent and invisible – it has no 'show-room' for its services equivalent to the publicity of the linear industrial economy at the point of sale. Economic actors and their clients are close; publicity is often local by owner-user mouth to owner-user ear. In promoting the circular industrial economy, the question arises who should be praising its advantages to the owner-users of objects, for it is them who take the decision to extend the service-live of, or dispose and replace, the objects they use.

The role of the point of sale has grown with specialisation and globalisation in production. Craftsmen selling their wares locally knew their clients; there was no need for distributors. With growing distance between producer and buyer, alienation increased and shops and salesmen became the go-betweens, absorbing about 25 per cent of the sales price. They in turn have been replaced

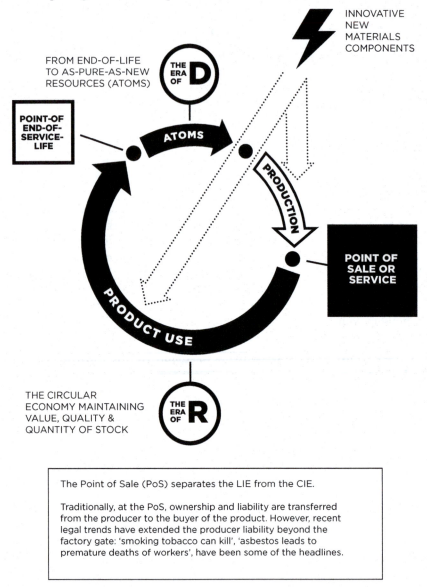

FROM END-OF-LIFE
TO AS-PURE-AS-NEW
RESOURCES (ATOMS)

THE ERA OF D

INNOVATIVE
NEW
MATERIALS
COMPONENTS

POINT-OF
END-OF-
SERVICE-
LIFE

ATOMS

PRODUCTION

PRODUCT USE

POINT OF
SALE OR
SERVICE

THE CIRCULAR
ECONOMY MAINTAINING
VALUE, QUALITY &
QUANTITY OF STOCK

THE ERA OF R

The Point of Sale (PoS) separates the LIE from the CIE.

Traditionally, at the PoS, ownership and liability are transferred from the producer to the buyer of the product. However, recent legal trends have extended the producer liability beyond the factory gate: 'smoking tobacco can kill', 'asbestos leads to premature deaths of workers', have been some of the headlines.

Figure 6.1 The key position of the point of sale between production and product use

by shopping centres, online websites and platforms like Uber, Airbnb and FlixBus – not without creating losers (Miller 1949).

Innovation at the point of sale is biased; the producer has the role of innovator, the buyer the role of selection. People wanting to buy an electric car had no choice, until Tesla appeared; its success shows that the latent demand has been there. People wanting to buy an easy to repair fridge will be unsatisfied if no manufacturer offers such an object; policymakers, however, can oblige manufacturers to produce such an object.

6.2 Of toys and tools, fashion and function

For consumer goods – toys – the point of sale is the pivot between production and use (Figure 6.1): objects produced in the linear industrial economy that cannot be sold will become zero-life goods (Figure 2.1), from food to books, computers, houses and power stations.

The point of sale is the most visible part of the linear industrial economy: annual shows and exhibitions of the latest cars, aircraft and books are the light-houses; publicity in print media, radio and TV and increasingly spots on the Internet is omnipresent. These are no longer Vance Packard's 'hidden persuaders' (Packard 1957) but audio-visual attacks on 'bystanders'. Influencers are the latest – and most efficient – method to reach specific audiences like children. Ryan, an eight-year-old American, gained US$22 million in 12 months. His show, Ryan-Toys-Review, has made him the top earner on YouTube, paid to unwrap and praise manufacturers' toys in front of his video camera, and then post the film on his YouTube channel. This is not a child working for a miserable wage in a mine in a less developed country – it is nevertheless a child working for big corporations, which probably state in their annual Corporate Social Responsibility report that they do not employ children, or procure anything from a source employing children.

For consumer goods – toys – the point of sale is passing the single message of buying new fashionable 'bigger-better-faster-safer-greener' goods. These are like 'toys' because their attractiveness disappears when new objects fulfilling the same function become available. Typical toys are garments, furniture, vehicles, sports equipment and consumer electronics like smartphones, which are mostly bought outright by individuals and disposed of after use.

For investment goods – tools – the point of sale is the pivot between man-ufacturing and a productive use, guided by functional criteria to maximise the expected return on investment. Typical tools are equipment operated by fleet managers in the Performance Economy (Chapter 8), such as railway companies and airlines, real estate managers, armed forces, rental businesses and leasing companies. Tools range from production equipment and real estate to cars, plants, artworks, uniforms and designer handbags. They are financial assets, which can be depreciated tax-wise. This depreciation may give economic incentives to extend the service-life of objects, or on the contrary to terminate their use once they are fully depreciated. Fleet managers and other professional owner-users of objects often have the knowledge and skills to repair and maintain, even to remanufacture their tools; this makes them champions of the circular industrial economy.

If economic actors retain the ownership of objects and sell goods as a service, the point of sale changes into the factory gate (for mobile goods) or the commissioning gate (for built objects) as border posts between manufacturers and a productive use.

Manufacturers and fleet managers now have full control over their service-life and the skills, knowledge and economic motivation to take preventive actions to extend the service-life of their objects. By internalising all liabilities and costs for losses and waste they treat all objects as 'tools' and fully exploit the opportunities of the eras of 'R' and 'D' to maximise profits.

Many items such as cars, computers or smartphones are 'dual-use' objects, where the use determines whether it has the characteristic of a tool or a toy (the term dual-use normally refers to objects, which can be used for military or civil purposes).

6.3 The point of sale: pivot for ownership and liability

At the point of sale, ownership and liability for use and end-of-life are transferred from producer to buyer, except for a warranty covering manufacturing defects during a limited period of time. Ownership of objects includes the right to reuse or remarket, the right to repair or upgrade – or to dispose of. The owner of the object controls the object's use and decides how long the object will 'live', and what 'R' services, do-it-yourself skills and such social schemes as repair cafés will be used to extend an object's service-life. A caring attitude and access to operation and maintenance (O&M) services of high quality are important, because with increasing product-life, O&M quality becomes more important than manufacturing quality.

The ownership–liability link is questioned by the digitalisation of the economy and the Internet of Things. For smart and autonomous goods, ownership tends to be split between hardware and software, with the producer of the software moving into the driver seat. For a number of reasons, such as quick revenues, manufacturers like Apple and John Deere still sell the hardware (smartphones and tractors) but refuse to give their customers access to the source codes and algorithms of the software, which would enable them to repair the technical systems and control and extend their service-life. If producers want to have the cake and eat it, curtailing the property rights of the system owner-user and aborting the service-life of objects, the ownership issue is fuzzy.

When ownership of the physical good is transferred, but ownership and control of the software is retained by the manufacturer, a conflict arises. This violates the circular industrial economy principle 'if you can't repair it, you don't own it', which means that producers should have no ownership rights on hardware and software after the point of sale. This situation has led to a 'right to repair' issue, which in 2018 was being fought in US courts by Kyle Wiens, CEO of iFixit. com, on a number of fronts. The company has not won any battles yet, but in 17 US states legislation has started to move, with iFixit gaining ground.[1]

EU Member States ruled at a 7 January 2019 meeting that spare parts for refrigerators have to be replaceable with the use of commonly available tools and without damaging the product. They also voted that spare parts be available for at least seven years, with parts such as door gaskets and trays available to end-users, and thermostats and temperature sensors available only to professional repair technicians; professional technicians have to receive access to repair information.

Selling smart goods exclusively as a service in the Performance Economy, with ownership and liability for both hard- and software remaining with the producer, avoids these issues (Chapter 8).

6.4 Producer liability is shifting

In the twenty-first century, 'diesel-gate' has cost some car manufacturers billions of US dollars in fines and forced buy-backs of cars, and may have accelerated the end of diesel engine production.

Cultural differences have appeared between the United States and Europe in interpreting manufacturers' liability. As a next step, producers may have to accept a liability for the end-of-life of their products, closing the Producer Liability loop (see Chapter 7). And there is a trend that the one-time point of sale will increasingly become a recurring point of service.

Already today, manufacturers selling performance and fleet managers selling goods as service (rental objects, public transport) or molecules as service (chemical leasing, rent a molecule) give a guarantee for the functioning of their products or even for the performance promised. The point of sale has become a point of user-service. Industrial designers working for these economic actors have now widely accepted eco-design (design for environment) principles of waste prevention and energy efficiency in order to maximise the profits of fleet managers. If the upcoming EU eco-design directive (www.coolproducts.eu/) comes into force, it could reinforce this trend in Europe.

The shift towards an Extended Producer Liability may well motivate manufacturers in the linear industrial economy to move to a circular industrial economy for reasons of competitiveness and in order to reduce potential liability. Policymakers and public procurement agencies could become major influencers in promoting such a shift by buying performance instead of objects.

6.5 What is in it for manufacturers, after the point of sale?

In the linear industrial economy, manufacturers optimise their supply chain up to the point of sale. As a longer use life of goods is equivalent to fewer sales, resulting in smaller production volumes, a lower economy of scale and higher unit costs, this option is poison to most producers' balance sheets. A shorter service-life of objects is inherently more interesting to manufacturers in today's policy framework.

The service-life of investment goods – tools – is determined by the owner-user, who is guided by the tax period to fully depreciate his investment. Manufacturers have a limited influence to speed up replacement sales as their only influence on tax depreciation rules is through lobbying. Offering technology upgrades for goods in use is of a lesser interest as it would create less revenue than selling new mass-produced objects and would demand a decentralised activity, which is diametrically opposed to centralised or even globalised manufacturing.

The service-life of consumer goods – toys – is also determined by the owner-user, but who is guided by his disposable income and his wishes. As the markets for many toys are near saturation, a shorter service-life of objects will enable higher sales volumes and is therefore inherently more interesting to manufacturers. One lever to achieve shorter service-lives of goods is to speed up sales at the point of sale, using publicity and marketing to sell the advantages of new goods. '*Vorsprung durch Technik*' (advancing through technology) has long been the slogan of a German manufacturer of premium automobiles.

Manufacturers offering free repairs for their goods, such as Patagonia, are among the rare exceptions.

However, integrating the knowledge of the circular industrial economy into the manufacturing process makes sense for manufacturers also remanufacturing their goods. A case in point is Caterpillar's diesel engines; Caterpillar no longer specifies if a new engine is new or remanufactured, as the technical specifications, sales price and warranty are the same. What has changed is that the design of new engines now takes into account features to reduce the costs of remanufacturing and technological upgrading processes.

As the only resource for remanufacturing are used objects, Caterpillar buys back broken engines from the owner-user, at a price which depends on the degree of non-destruction of the broken engine. The answer to the question asked in Figure 5.2 is in this case that all actors involved profit from reuse at the highest value preservation level. The question of who should be praising the advantages of the circular industrial economy no longer arises if manufacturers are also actors of the circular industrial economy, and the profits from service-life extension are shared by owner-user and (re)manufacturer.

Note

1   https://repair.org/legislation, accessed 23 January 2019. iFixit's biggest win in 2018 relates to software; https://motherboard.vice.com/en_us/article/xw9bwd/1201-exemptions-right-to-repair, accessed 23 January 2019.

References

Miller, Henry (1949 [1976]) *Death of a salesman*. Penguin Plays, London.
Packard, Vance (1957) *The hidden persuaders*. Longman Green and Company, London.

7 The invisible liability loop, labour and the role of policy

The liability for end-of-service-life objects and materials ('waste') is with the last owner, for consumer goods – toys – often municipalities. By defining waste as 'objects without positive value or ultimate liable owner', policies introducing an Extended Producer Liability which includes objects at the end of their service life would create an individual rather than collective accountability for waste. Changes in taxation, carbon credits and jumps in technology could further promote the circular industrial economy.

7.1 Extended Producer Liability (EPL): closing the invisible liability loop

The centre of the circular economy is YOU, the policymaker:

- If you introduce policy instruments, which oblige producers and sellers to take back their goods if they have no positive value and no liable owner at the end of the service-life, then you are boosting the circular industrial economy. The same is true if you create legal instruments obliging producers and sellers of materials to buy-back or take-back their used materials and to recover pure atoms and molecules to be remarketed.

The sustainability impact of the circular industrial economy can be greatly enhanced by closing the invisible liability loops both for objects and materials (Figure 7.1), in addition to closing the physical loops of objects in the era of 'R' and of molecules in the era of 'D'.

In the linear industrial economy, liability for the use of objects lies with the user-owner of goods. Weapon manufacturers maintain that guns do not kill, the person pulling the trigger does. But this manufacturer strategy of the linear industrial economy, to limit producer liability after the point of sale to short warranty periods, has started to fade in the second half of the twentieth century. Nestlé was accused of 'potentially harming babies' by selling milk powder in less developed countries without detailed instructions on how to prepare drinks using infant formula; the tobacco industry was accused of killing smokers and even passive smokers through its products; and the asbestos industry of

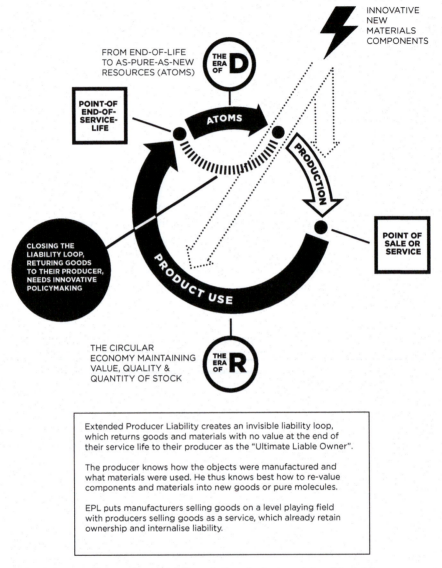

INNOVATIVE
NEW
MATERIALS
COMPONENTS

FROM END-OF-LIFE
TO AS-PURE-AS-NEW
RESOURCES (ATOMS)

THE ERA OF **D**

POINT-OF
END-OF-
SERVICE-
LIFE

ATOMS

PRODUCTION

CLOSING THE
LIABILITY LOOP,
RETURING GOODS
TO THEIR PRODUCER,
NEEDS INNOVATIVE
POLICYMAKING

PRODUCT USE

POINT OF
SALE OR
SERVICE

THE CIRCULAR
ECONOMY MAINTAINING
VALUE, QUALITY &
QUANTITY OF STOCK

THE ERA OF **R**

Extended Producer Liability creates an invisible liability loop,
which returns goods and materials with no value at the end of
their service life to their producer as the "Ultimate Liable Owner".

The producer knows how the objects were manufactured and
what materials were used. He thus knows best how to re-value
components and materials into new goods or pure molecules.

EPL puts manufacturers selling goods on a level playing field
with producers selling goods as a service, which already retain
ownership and internalise liability.

Figure 7.1 Extended Producer Liability: closing the immaterial and invisible
        liability loop

causing the death of workers having produced or worked with asbestos cement
goods, even decades after the end of the production. The movement could
now spread to services, such as the gambling industry and even, in the eyes of
some people, 'social media as the new cigarette'. This could herald tougher
legislation and punitive fines for producers, especially in the United States.

Yet this development is less revolutionary than it may sound. It continues
the philosophy of the 1976 US Resource Conservation and Recovery Act, the

1980 US Superfund legislation and the Polluter Pays Principle (PPP), which was first mentioned in the OECD recommendation of 26 May 1972 and reaffirmed in the recommendation of 14 November 1974. It makes the party responsible for producing pollution also responsible for paying for the damage done to the natural environment. In 2003, European policymakers imposed an Extended Producer Responsibility (EPR) on manufacturers and importers of electronic and electric objects (EU 2003). But this EPR is only financial, typically a small fee added at the point of sale. The responsibility for the end-of-service-life can be delegated to third party waste managers. But as the latter have no access to producer knowledge and lack the expertise – or by contractual obligations are not allowed – to exploit the highest value conservation option of reusing components or materials, they aim for the cheapest recycling or disposal methods, thus waiving the opportunities in Figure 5.2.

As a result, only few electrical and electronic equipment (EEE) producers have changed their industrial design priorities or installed buy-back strategies to recover goods, components or molecules for reuse.

7.2 Objects: EPL and Ultimate Liable Owners in the era of 'R'

The present policy framework of the circular industrial economy, such as the EU's Circular Economy Package, aims to close the highly visible material loops of the era of 'R'. It misses a major driver to reach sustainability by closing the liability loop through an Extended Producer Liability.

Defining waste as 'objects without positive value or ultimate liable owner' opens up:

- industrial solutions – use materials with inherent value, such as gold or copper, to give used objects a positive value – and;
- policy solutions – define the original producer as the Ultimate Liable Owner.

Closing the liability loop means that goods with no value at the end of their service-life can be returned to their producer as Ultimate Liable Owner (ULO). The author has derived the concept of the ULO from that of the Ultimate Beneficial Owner (UBO), which was introduced in the United States in the 1980s to reduce tax evasion through chain ownerships of companies in tax havens.

An Extended Producer Liability will give producers strong incentives to prevent future liabilities by designing goods for maximum end-of-service-life value and minimum liability. Extended Producer Liability furthermore puts manufacturers selling goods on a level playing field with economic actors selling goods as a service that already retain the ownership and liability of their objects and materials over the full service-life.

The objective of the circular industrial economy is to maintain the highest value and utility of manufactured objects, for instance through reuse and service-life extension strategies. A number of developments could accelerate the introduction of an Extended Producer Liability, such as:

- if the objective of law is to protect victims, and considering the digitalisation of the economy and the absence of a liable 'owner-user' in smart goods, an Extended Producer Liability for systems would protect users (consumers) and the environment;
- if the objective is to achieve zero waste, the producers of manufactured objects, who designed and produced them and whose name or code is shown on the product, know best how the object was constructed, what materials were used, how the objects can be dismantled and materials reused. In addition, the producer controls the value added and distribution chains, fixes the sales price and can internalise the end of life costs into the price at the point of sale. Producers are thus the logical 'Ultimate Liable Owners' of their objects.

Applying an Ultimate Liable Owner responsibility to tools – manufactured objects used by economic actors to create revenue (such as machine tools, commercial vehicles, production equipment) – reinforces the owner's present responsibility for end-of-service-life costs and his economic interest in achieving the highest reuse value by selling:

- components suitable for remanufacture, e.g. bearings, to the original equipment manufacturer (OEM);
- materials suitable for molecule recovery, e.g. ferrous and non-ferrous metals, to resource managers; or
- buildings, or the land on which they stand, to a developer.

Applying an Ultimate Liable Owner responsibility to toys – manufactured objects owned and used by individuals – changes the present responsibility for end-of-service-life costs (collection and disposal) with municipalities or recyclers. For toys that have a negative value, municipalities and nation states today become the waste owners and managers of last resort. Typical examples are abandoned objects in municipal waste streams and plastic in the oceans.

Toys is where the concepts of Extended Producer Liability and Ultimate Liable Owner will bite most; they will give producers a strong incentive to avoid a liability for future products. However, the concept of Extended Producer Liability will only tackle the legacy problems, such as plastic in the oceans, if applied retroactively, similar to the tobacco and asbestos cases.

7.3 Materials: EPL and Ultimate Liable Owners in the era of 'D'

The objective of the circular industrial economy is to maintain the highest value and purity of stocks of atoms and molecules. But the objective of traditional end-of-pipe recycling activities is to minimise recyclers' costs, not to retain the highest material value for society. This clash between micro- and macro-economic optimisation today leads to substantial macro-economic losses, despite high recycling rates. In Sweden, a recent report with a value perspective on material recycling (Material Economics 2018) analyses the use of materials in the Swedish economy in monetary terms instead of tonnes and cubic metres. Aluminium and steel recycling rates of 85 per cent (measured in tonnes), compare with retained value rates of 40 per cent (measured in SEK) after one use cycle. For plastics, a recycling rate of 53 per cent in tonnes compares with a retained value rate of 15 per cent. The report seeks to answer questions such as: For each 100 SEK of raw material entering the Swedish economy, how much value is retained after one use cycle? What are the main reasons that material value is lost? What measures could retain more materials value, and how much could be recovered? What business opportunities arise as a result?

An Extended Producer Liability, *defining waste as materials without positive value or Ultimate Liable Owner*, would give producers of manufactured materials, such as metal alloys and polymers, strong incentives to design molecules, which can be identified and recovered through sorting technologies, in order to maintain a positive value and prevent future liabilities.

Note that the concepts of Ultimate Liable Owner and Extended Producer Liability will not solve the problem of molecules ending up in 'free' waste dumps, such as the atmosphere (CO_2 and other GHG emissions), oceans (micro plastic and toxic chemicals) and space (abandoned satellites and space-craft). This problem, known as 'Tragedy of the Commons' (Hardin 1968), today also embraces natural capital, biodiversity, biogenetics and society's knowledge pool and demands international political action.

7.4 Labour in the circular economy: a suitable case for research

Few research studies or publications have looked at the impact of time on pro-duction factors (Giarini and Stahel 1989).[1] An obvious obstacle to research in this topic is time itself: how to analyse the labour input in the use of an automobile over 30 years, for example, for a PhD thesis? By the time the student has finished his thesis, he has nearly reached the age of retirement. Many fleet managers use equipment over long periods of time – witness the B52 bombers from 1952, or the 30-year-old Airforce One – but may not keep the data over the full service-life. Railways typically delete service-life data of rolling stock after each general overhaul to 'as good as new' condition. As a result, data that could be used to justify political decisions in favour of a shift to a circular industrial economy is rare and can easily be ignored as not representative.

This aspect of research will gain in importance in the future with the shift to long-life technologies, sketched in Section 10.2.

One existing analysis of total expenses – total monies spent excluding fuel and insurance – over a service-life period of 30 years was done by the author for his car (Bierter *et al.* 1999; Figure 7.2).[2] As could be expected, the factory's share continuously diminishes, whereas the share of labour costs constantly increases:

- from 18 per cent after ten years,
- to 34 per cent after 20 years, and
- 48 per cent after 30 years.

> An extended service-life of objects thus clearly corresponds to a substitution of local labour for energy and materials consumed in production. Other cost factors, such as oil and parts, remain relatively constant. Not taxing labour would thus make service-life extension activities more competitive. The car is still in use today, especially for oldtimer events; it can be expected that labour costs will reach a glass ceiling around 75 per cent of total costs.

In this case – a Toyota produced in Japan, used and serviced in Switzerland – service-life extension also means that Swiss car mechanics have replaced Japanese factory workers.

7.5 The role of policy and labour taxation

Policymakers are struggling with a number of global problems, which are grouped under the umbrella of Sustainable Development Goals (SDG). Defined by the United Nations in 2015, 17 global goals cover a broad range of social and economic development issues.

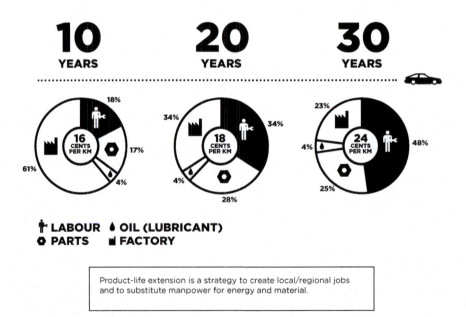

Figure 7.2 Analysis of the running costs of a car over a 30-year period

Through the circular industrial economy's characteristic of high-labour but low carbon and low-resource input, and its strong reliance on small and medium-size decentralised enterprises, policies to promote the circular industrial economy contribute to many of the SDGs in a holistic way. To appreciate the contribution of the circular industrial economy to the SDGs, the 17 separate goals or 'silos' and 169 targets need to be replaced by a holistic or performance approach.

Take 'sustainable taxation' (Stahel 2013), a concept which considers the relative weight of labour and material resources as production factors. It greatly differs in the linear and the circular industrial economy:

- the linear industrial economy is resource- and capital-intensive, with a high labour productivity equal to a small labour input;
- the circular industrial economy is labour-intensive, with a high resource productivity equal to a minor consumption of material, water and energy resources.

In many countries, today's fiscal policies heavily tax labour and subsidise the production and consumption of fossil fuels and other non-renewable resources – the opposite of sustainability.

Reversing this situation, by not taxing renewable resources like human labour and taxing non-renewable ones instead, would give individuals and economic actors direct incentives to shift towards the circular industrial economy, managing their belongings instead of replacing them with new ones. It would motivate people to 'build ships' in Saint-Exupéry's image.

Economic success does not depend on income taxes. Florida and Texas, two powerhouses of the US economy, are among the 11 US states that do not tax labour income and yet flourish economically. And human labour is a renewable low-waste low-carbon resource; taxing non-renewable resources instead will:

- speed up the transformation from flow to stock optimisation, from the linear to the circular industrial economy;
- broaden the application of the circular economy to new economic actors and new sectors; and
- strengthen the competitiveness of the existing economic actors of the circular industrial economy as well as of all other activities involving caring, such as health, education and looking after natural and cultural capitals.

Sustainable taxation should also respect the nature of the circular economy by:

- not charging Value Added Tax (VAT) in Europe on such value preserving activities as reuse, repair and remanufacture (without value added); and
- giving carbon credits for the prevention of greenhouse gas (GHG) emissions to the same degree as for their reduction, considering activities of the era of 'R' as CDM projects (see Chapter 10).

The era of 'R' and partly the era of 'D' prevent large GHG emissions (and waste) but receive no carbon credits under any of the existing or planned CO_2 compensation programmes, which are based on the linear thinking of today's industrial economy: first pollute, then be rewarded for reducing pollution!

Adapting the framework conditions to this fact has begun in some countries. At the end of 2016, the Swedish parliament decided to half VAT levied on repairs and to make the labour costs of repairs deductible from income tax. At the 2017 EU summit in Luxembourg, EU Commissioner for Finance Moscovici suggested that all EU Member States, which have sole authority to change national taxation policy, do the same. A halt to subsidising the production and consumption of fossil fuels is part of the same strategy.

Depreciation rules strongly influence the service-life of investment goods, or tools. Governments can therefore promote the transition to the circular industrial economy through longer fiscal depreciation periods. The long average service-life of aircraft stems from fiscal depreciation periods of 15 years, which entails a product liability by manufacturers of 18–22 years. There is a strong correlation between the service-life of goods, manufacturers' liability periods and tax depreciation periods (Stahel 2010, pp. 185–186). Legislators can use longer tax depreciation and product liability periods as a policy to create jobs at home, prevent waste and boost regional economic development.

Policymakers will increasingly be challenged to adapt existing policies to changes in the real world. Use value as the new central economic value of the circular economy demands a redefinition of compensations in third party liability, for instance in insurance contracts, replacing depreciated value. The emergence of long-life technologies calls for equally long tax depreciation periods, in order to prevent service-life abortion for corporate tax reasons; efforts to halt global climate change calls for recognition of the CO_2 emission prevention by the circular economy and rewarding its economic actors with carbon compensation credits (see Chapter 10).

Public procurement policies are another approach for governments to speed up the shift to a circular industrial economy, both as major buyer-owners of objects and through subsidies to buyer-owners. Public procurement and public subsidies together have an impact on about 35 per cent of the GDP of industrialised countries.

7.6 The role of appropriate economic indicators

By introducing absolute decoupling indicators (Figure 7.3), governments can make the impact of changes visible to policymakers, economic actors and consumers. The 2000 EU Lisbon strategy[3] stated as objectives more wealth, more jobs and lower resource consumption, which coincides with the aims of the circular industrial economy. Figure 7.3 puts these factors into perspective and shows the two absolute decoupling indicators that can be derived:

- value per weight, in euro per kilogram (€/kg);
- labour input per weight, in hour per kilogram (hr/kg).

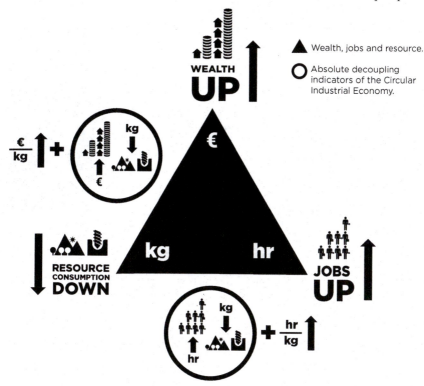

Figure 7.3 The two absolute decoupling indicators of the circular industrial economy monitoring more wealth and jobs from less resource consumption

These indicators can be used to compare the sustainability of products commercialised through different business models, measured at the point of sale in 'net €/kg' and 'net hr/kg' (Stahel 2006, pp. 62 and 127). Kilograms and hours refer to the resources invested in the relevant processes and embodied in the objects; reuse of an object needs zero kilogram.

Sustainability performance ratings of economic sectors can now be derived using these two absolute decoupling indicators (Figure 7.4).[4] Comparing typical manufactured objects and activities of the linear and the circular industrial economy shows two distinct clusters of economic activities:

- the linear industrial economy with low hr/kg (labour input per weight) ratios, coherent with mass production in highly mechanised processes, and low to medium €/kg (value per weight) ratios, in a range from basic materials like cement to smart goods like USB memory sticks;
- the circular industrial economy with much higher hr/kg and €/kg ratios for reuse, remanufacture and selling performance (goods as a service), in a group with new technologies, such as life sciences and nanotechnologies, which by nature produce dematerialised objects.

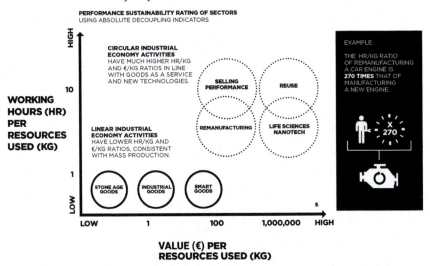

Figure 7.4 Absolute decoupling indicators make the difference between the linear industrial economy and the circular industrial economy visible

Some exceptionally high-value goods, such as diamonds and saffron, an agricultural produce, are situated outside the diagram.

7.7 The role of governments and policymakers

If a government wants to contribute to making the circular industrial economy the default option for manufactured objects and materials, it:

* will have to overcome a transition phase of contradicting objectives;
* can choose from several policy options; and
* has to quantify and sell the winnings.

In the transition phase from the present dominating linear to a circular industrial economy, there will be a competition of the two systems, such as globalised production versus intelligent decentralised services. In a mature circular industrial economy, production will have become an integral part of the former (see Figure 3.3). Communicating the vision of a mature circular industrial economy from the very beginning will be crucial; showing its close relation with accepted trends, such as organic farming, intelligent decentralisation and zero waste, will ease oppositions to the transition.

A number of policy options are available:

* spreading the knowledge of the opportunities offered by the circular industrial economy through education and information;

- leading the way through public procurement policies to speed up and broaden the shift to a circular industrial economy;
- not taxing renewable resources including labour, and taxing virgin non-renewable resources instead, would motivate individuals to preserve their belongings rather than replace them, for the simple reason that repairs are cheaper than buying new;
- longer fiscal depreciation periods and depreciation beyond zero would motivate many corporates to extend the service-life of their tools, thus creating jobs, preventing waste, boosting innovation into technological upgrading options and promoting regional economic development without top-down governance.

A multitude of winnings will result from the shift to a circular industrial economy, ranging from substantially reduced GHG emissions, the creation of skilled jobs locally – also for 'silver' and manual workers – and a reindustrialisation of regions, to the preservation of the cultural capital and technical heritage of regions.

To quantify, document and sell these winnings, governments will need to adopt novel reporting tools, such as absolute decoupling indicators, reports on the increasing wealth of the nation in natural, human, cultural, manufactured and financial assets or capitals, as well as revising existing ones, such as Input/Output models (Wijkman and Skanberg 2016). The World Bank has started to periodically publish reports on the changes of the wealth of nations for a number of countries (World Bank Group 2018).

Other efforts to quantify, document and sell the winnings of a shift to a circular industrial economy are possible for specific topics, such as emission reductions and resource preservation. However, to grasp the wealth of these winnings, policymakers will have to develop and communicate in more holistic ways than today.

Today's focus on waste minimisation needs to shift to resource preservation, giving priority to promoting:

- reuse and longer service-life options (the era of 'R'), as stipulated in the 2015 EU Circular Economy Package;
- the development of methods to collect and sort clean material fractions; and
- the development of technologies to recover molecules and atoms (the era of 'D')

In the era of 'D', a novel policy approach is needed to measure the annual resource efficiency of fast-moving flows. Legislation should define the maximum acceptable annual value loss of a resource stock instead of the minimal recycling rates for two reasons:

- recovery processes with an efficiency of 50 per cent conserve 50 per cent of material stock; in serial recycling, this means that 50 per cent of the material is preserved in the first loop, 25 per cent in the second and only 12.5 per cent in the third – what the author calls the 'reverse compound principle'.

- If the object involved has a ten year service-life, such as a combustion engine, that means an annual material loss of 5 per cent. But if the object is a drink can with a one-month service-life, the total resource stock has been lost after only six months, despite a recycling rate of 50 per cent.
- maximal acceptable annual value loss because the economic losses (in monetary terms) due to the loss of quality are considerably higher than the material quantity losses (in tonnages or volume). Only the former represent changes in societal wealth.

This policy change will call for new 'D' approaches and technologies. Who should pay for these, which will primarily benefit the environment, secondly improve national resource security? Following the Polluter Pays Principle, the logic answer is: the producers. An Extended Producer Liability wold give manufacturers strong financial incentives to change the choice of materials, or the strategy of commercialising objects to retain ownership and thus be able to recover products after use.

A recent Swedish study arrived at the following conclusions:

> Policy will have a central role in achieving improved handling of materials. A first step could be to re-examine pre-existing policies. Current targets for materials collection could be reformulated to take aim at secondary materials production and material value instead. The current 'producer responsibility' framework creates weak or non-existent incentives, but could be steered towards some degree of individual rather than collective accountability, underpinned by new technology for the marking and tracking of products. Without the introduction of these types of policies, secondary material will continue to face an uphill battle. Today's playing field is far from level, and therefore other types of measures may also be required – such as requirements for the use of recycled material (recovered molecules) in new products. International cooperation will be crucial. Most products and materials are international commodities, and it is necessary to coordinate policies, first and foremost at EU level (the European Commission took an important first step with the 2015 Circular Economy Package, but its implementation now requires additional initiatives).
>
> (Material Economics 2018)

Notes

1 Among the exceptions is the book *The limits to certainty, facing risks in the new service economy* (Giarini and Stahel 1989).
2 Prices not adjusted for inflation.

3 In March 2000, the European Council in Lisbon set out a ten-year strategy to make the Union 'the most competitive and dynamic knowledge-based economy in the world, capable of sustainable economic growth, with more and better jobs and greater social cohesion'. Under the strategy, a stronger economy will drive job creation alongside social and environmental policies that ensure sustainable development and social inclusion.

4 Source: http://product-life.org/en/major-publications/performance-economy, accessed 20 March 2019.

References

Bierter, Willy, Buhrow, Julian and Stahel, Walter R. (1999) Langzeit-Kostenanalyse von Fahrzeugen (PKW und LKW) (LCA of cars and trucks). http://product-life.org/de/archive/case-studies/langzeit-kostenanalyse-von-fahrzeugen-pkw-und-lkw, accessed 9 January 2019.

EU 2003 WEEE Directive (2003) European Community Directive 2012/19/EU on waste electrical and electronic equipment (WEEE) which, together with the RoHS Directive 2011/65/EU, became European Law in February 2003.

Giarini, Orio and Stahel, Walter R. (1989) *The limits to certainty, facing risks in the new service economy.* Kluwer Academic Publishers, Dordrecht.

Hardin, Garret (1968) Tragedy of the commons. *Science*, vol. 162, no. 3859, pp. 1243–1248.

Material Economics (2018) Ett värdebeständigt svenskt materialsystem (Retaining value in the Swedish materials system). Economic value measured in billion Swedish Kroner versus material measured in tonnes. Research study, unpublished.

Stahel, Walter (2006) *The performance economy*, first edition. Palgrave Macmillan, Houndmills.

Stahel, Walter (2010) *The performance economy,* second edition. Palgrave Macmillan, Houndmills.

Stahel, Walter (2013) Policy for material efficiency: Sustainable taxation as a departure from the throwaway society. *Philosophical Transactions A of the Royal Society*, vol. 371, pp. 1–19.

Wijkman, Anders and Skanberg, Kristian (2016) *The circular economy and benefits for society jobs and climate clear winners in an economy based on renewable energy and resource efficiency.* The Club of Rome, Winterthur. www.clubofrome.org/wp-content/uploads/2016/03/The-Circular-Economy-and-Benefits-for-Society.pdf, accessed 9 January 2019.

World Bank Group (2018) The changing wealth of nations report 2018. https://openknowledge.worldbank.org/bitstream/handle/10986/29001/9781464810466.pdf, accessed 9 January 2019.

8 The Performance Economy, industry adopting the circular industrial economy as default option

The Performance Economy is profitable, ecologically and socially viable and induces innovation, but there is no sharing without caring. Producers of manufactured materials and objects can take a leading role by renting or leasing their molecules and goods, in combination with efficient return logistic loops. By including the factor 'Time' in economic optimisation, new opportunities open up in the use of objects. Public procurement of buying performance acts as initiator for innovative circular industrial economy start-ups.

8.1 The business models

The centre of the circular economy is YOU, the manager of a fleet of objects.

- If you properly maintain and sell your objects as a service for the longest possible time, then you are part of the Performance Economy.
- If you re-market surplus equipment and used objects at the end of their service-life, or dismantle them and sell components that are used but not broken, then you participate in the circular industrial economy. The same is true if you sell the broken components to somebody else to repair them or recover the atoms and molecules.

The Performance Economy sells results instead of objects. Its economic actors may be manufacturers of durable objects or fleet managers operating them. In both cases, they sell the use of these objects as a service over the longest possible period of time and maximise their profits by exploiting both efficiency and sufficiency solutions. In comparison to the circular industrial economy, the fields of application of the Performance Economy are broader and include single-use products, such as chemicals and pharmaceuticals.

The Performance Economy of selling goods and molecules as a service, function guarantees or results and performance (Figure 8.1), is the most sustainable business model of the circular industrial economy because by internalising the costs of product liability, of risk and waste, it offers manufacturers a strong financial incentive to prevent losses and waste. It maximises the profit potential by exploiting sufficiency, efficiency and systems solutions. In addition,

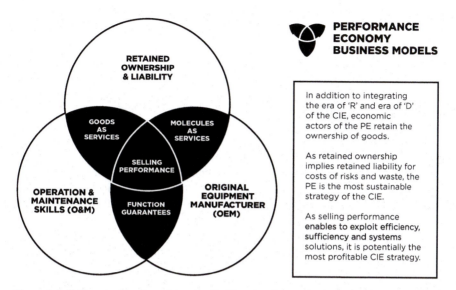

Figure 8.1 Selling performance instead of selling goods: combining Original Equipment Manufacturer (OEM) and Operation and Maintenance (O&M) skills with retained ownership.

by maintaining the ownership of objects and embodied resources, it creates long-term corporate and national resource security at low cost.

8.2 The decision makers

The Performance Economy redefines the role of the supply side, but also implies a radical change of the demand side, from owner-ship to user-ship of objects. Is this cultural shift really new? Aristotle had already stated that real wealth lies in the use, not the ownership of goods, two thousand years ago.

The dominating economic model in industrialised countries throughout the twentieth and most of the twenty-first century has been geared towards individual ownership and disposability of goods, and the wish to own the 'next big thing'. In recent years, we have seen a trend away from this model towards one centred on the desirability of access to goods and services. In the last decade, many young people have stopped aspiring to have a driver's licence or own a car, partly because they fear the costs involved and the liability incurred on today's congested roads. They do not have the money to buy real estate property, but owning a smartphone of the latest generation is a must for most, as is permanent availability through cheap communication services. Potential risks involved for health and privacy are ignored.

In a rental economy, users do not need capital to access goods,[1] but they do not profit from capital gains either. For individuals, owning goods makes economic sense for goods that increase in value over time; owning real estate makes sense, owning a smartphone or washing machine does not. By renting objects, users gain flexibility in use, know the cost of using a product in advance and only pay when using it. Individuals with a weakness for fashion and constant change can fully live their fancies without causing excess waste by renting every weekend a different fashionable sports car, outfit or handbag from economic actors managing stocks (fleets) of these objects.

Fleet managers prefer objects of high quality and low-maintenance cost, focusing on function not short-lived fashion. They also have the knowledge to optimise operation and minimise maintenance costs of their stocks of objects, for example through standardised components and technical systems as well as a cascading use of objects. Xerox very early imposed its commonality principle, specifying the same 'common' components across its equipment range. Airbus introduced from the beginning a standardised flight deck for all its aircraft, saving airlines operation and maintenance costs in crew training, stand-by crews and parts management.

Textile leasing companies rent uniforms, hotel and sterile hospital textiles; they only make profits once the fabrics and garments have been in use for more than three years. They therefore avoid fashion trends and use high quality repairable fabrics, which are easy to clean and maintain. As their operation is geographically limited by transport costs, and the knowledge of clients' needs is vital, they operate through regional franchises, not centralisation. Real estate owners are often life insurance companies or family trusts interested in steady income flows, long-term value preservation and low operation and maintenance costs. These can best be achieved through a high initial quality of materials and objects and a familiarity with local customs and conditions.

Detailed knowledge of operation and maintenance is also necessary for facility managers in charge of building or operating complex infrastructures, such as airports or bridges. The French company Eiffage in 2001 signed a 78-year contract to design, finance, build and operate until 2079 a viaduct near Millau, with a maintenance contract running until 2121. The project is a Private Finance Initiative (PFI); the bridge did not cost the French taxpayer a single euro, but each vehicle crossing the bridge has to pay a toll (as the bridge deck is more than 200 meters above the valley, pedestrians are not allowed to cross in order to prevent suicides). Risks are carried by, and profits go to, Eiffage who will know at the latest 78 years after the signature of the contract how much loss or profit it has made. Whereas pure risks (accidents) can be insured, entrepreneurial risks (management mistakes) cannot; risk management becomes a key corporate capability in the Performance Economy.

Innovation in the Performance Economy comes from a shift of focus, from optimising production to optimising the utilisation of objects and molecules, and from including the factor time in this optimisation (see Figure 8.5). Analysing the use or utilisation of objects opens up new opportunities, such as long-life goods, service strategies, system solutions and multifunctional goods. The latter, such as all-in-one printer-copier-scanner-fax machines, have become common with the digitalisation of technology. These opportunities are of little interest for manufacturing industries selling objects, but profitably exploited by actors selling goods as a service. Examples are:

- Goods sold as a service for exclusive use comprise rental apartments, tools and vehicles for rent, but also books in public libraries, public toilets, ISO shipping containers and leased equipment and reusable packaging.
- Goods or systems sold as a service for shared use embrace all forms of public transport (busses, trains, ferries, aircraft), as well as public swimming pools, concert halls and laundromats.
- Business to Business examples include ceramic slide-gate services for the steel and iron industry, maintenance-free crude oil pumps, DuPont performance coating services, power by the hour for gas turbines and jet engines by Rolls-Royce and tyres by the mile by Michelin for haulage companies. Molecules as a service are chemical leasing contracts (also called rent a molecule), which enable a precise accounting of the losses of chemicals into the environment between lessor and lessee, which is legally required for Toxic Release Inventories. UNIDO promotes chemical leasing as a strategy for Africa, in order to minimise pollution and toxic packaging waste in industrially less developed regions. Dow Chemical, through its subsidiary Safe-Chem, has been leasing solvents for many years.
- An example of function guarantees are maintenance contracts for lifts. Vertical lifts and cable cars have a catastrophic risk potential in case of failure; national safety legislations therefore impose the provision of automatic brake systems and periodic check-ups to prevent accidents. These services can be supplied by manufacturers and local specialised third party service providers.

For catalytic goods, which are contaminated but not consumed during use, such as lubrication oils, an integrated 'rent-a-molecule' service enables economic actors to create revenue without resource consumption (Stahel 2010, p. 87). An international agreement to stop the production of mercury after 2020 could lead to closed loop and rental strategies in the future commercialisation of mercury.

Business models of rent-a-molecule demand a fundamental redefinition of contractual obligations between manufacturers, distributors and users.

Strategies of molecules as a service are not limited to chemicals with a catalytic function or high toxicity. Metal leasing is proposed by two scientists, Andrew Hagan and Michael Tost (2019), as a strategy for mining companies and governments of mining regions. Renting molecules, instead of selling ores, would give both a smaller short-term income but guarantee constant long-term revenues. Developing innovative smart materials will give material companies the same opportunity. The UK's Cookson Group developed a composite powder that can be pressed into any form and, when magnetised, becomes an extremely powerful permanent magnet. The two characteristics, easy shaping and magnetisation on demand, make it an ideal material for use as a rotor in small electric motors. After use, this smart material demagnetises when ground back into its powder form and can then be remixed for its next use. To exclusively benefit from the successive life-cycles of its smart materials, Cookson rents the material to component manufacturers, which have to guarantee its return. In this case, the strategy of selling performance must be imposed on all levels from material to component to product, to guarantee that the smart material is returned to its manufacturer at the end of the final product's life (Stahel 2010, p. 109).

These business model conditions are summarised in Figure 8.2, with the return logistics loops:

- back to the manufacturers of goods for used objects; and
- back to the materials producers for used molecules.

An early champion of this strategy mix since the early 1990s has been Xerox Corporation in the United States and Europe, and Ricoh-Xerox in Japan. Equipment is leased on a "pay per page produced" basis; ownership and liability are retained by Xerox. Used equipment is remanufactured and technologically updated in its regional factories; materials from components which cannot be remanufactured or reused in new equipment are returned to the original material producer, enabling a zero-waste operation (Harvard Business School 1994).

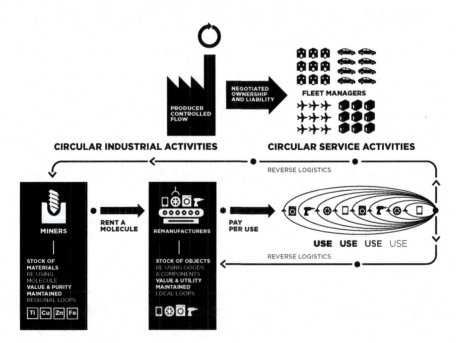

Figure 8.2 The Performance Economy

In selling goods as a service, economic actors retain ownership and liability, while users must show a caring attitude, a stewardship towards the rented objects. The frontier between owners and users varies; renting a car to go from A to B leaves users with a higher risk but gives them a higher flexibility than using a bus or aircraft. If a vehicle breaks down, responsibility in both cases is with the owner.

Selling performance is characterised by the fact that users pay a price per use, fixed in advance. This business model is widely accepted today by players of the linear industrial economy, and increasingly by individuals.

Public procurement buying performance acts as initiator for innovative start-ups. NASA's decision to rely on a rocket launch services programme, instead of owning and operating hardware (Space Shuttles) itself, led to the foundation of Space X, Odyssey Moon and other companies who are now successfully competing for space transport contracts with hardware and system solution of a novel type, such as reusable rockets using standardised components in a modular system.

8.3 The characteristics of the Performance Economy

The Performance Economy is the most sustainable business model of the circular industrial economy because selling performance improves sustainability in a holistic way: higher profits or lower costs, less resource consumption, more skilled labour input:

- Profitable because the Performance Economy exploits sufficiency, efficiency and systems solutions and, in comparison to both the linear and circular industrial economy, has fewer transaction and compliance costs and is not subject to carbon taxes or import duties on resources. Profitability rises through:

  - a more intensive use of rental objects;
  - selling results using sufficiency: tilling at night prevents 90 per cent of weeds from germinating; green vineyards use sheep instead of chemicals to control vegetation; IT server farms located in the far North can do without air conditioning, which − compared to IT in temperate climates − saves half the total energy in use;
  - pay for performance: Bayer sells precision farming services instead of chemicals; Novartis and Gilead offer novel cancer therapies − CAR-T-Cell therapies − in the United States and the EU. These genetically modified cells have to be produced individually for each patient and administered in qualified clinics. Novartis charges almost half a million US$ per patient, if successful. If the treatment fails partly or completely, the money is returned.
  - Systems innovation: GPS controlled autonomous vehicles with intelligent optics enable precision seeding, weeding, watering and harvesting in agriculture.

- Ecologically beneficial because the Performance Economy minimises the need for consumables, transport and packaging by fully exploiting the local reuse and service-life extension of objects.

    Michelin's fleet solution service—tyre use by the mile—uses mobile workshops to repair and re-groove tyres at client premises in combination with regional retreating plants. These measures reduce the demand for new tyres; local service activities will increasingly replace global tyre production plants.

- Socially viable because it is labour-intensive and internalises producer and user liability as well as the costs of risk and waste, which in the linear industrial economy are externalised and borne by society. In addition, Performance Economy activities reward stewardship and punish abuse, creating a caring attitude of users.

    Performance Economy services are labour- and skill-intensive by nature: the non-destructive and value-preserving disassembly of used objects, necessary periodically to guarantee performance, demands a qualitative judgement at each step; so does the critical analysis of the repair or remanufacture potential for dismantled components.

8.4 No sharing without caring: culture enters the economic game

Sharing and caring are concepts lacking in the linear industrial economy. Individuals therefore often have little experience of caring for objects in an economic context, except for their own belongings. But – in addition to managing manufactured assets – caring is key in successfully managing natural, cultural and human capital, such as education and health systems, which are typical for the circular economy and society.

Caring is a key requirement in the Performance Economy, based on a shared use of objects, either serial (hotel beds, taxis) or jointly (public transport, sports centres). Designing fail-safe and fool-proof objects is a new challenge. These topics were already discussed at the 1992 International Design Forum in Ulm, 'Common utilisation instead of singular consumption: A new relationship with goods' (IFG 1993).

Fleet managers can strengthen caring for objects used under their control, such as aircrafts operated by professional pilots, through technical strategies, such as an industrial design of long-life, low-maintenance objects and preventive maintenance.

Objects sold as a service and used by third parties outside the fleet managers' control is a different kettle of fish, be it 'free float' rental apartments or cars, or in the future autonomous vehicles. Such a 'shared Performance Economy' can be successful if built on trust, caring and shared responsibility. For rental durable objects, for instance, owners retain ownership and liability for the goods and assume that users will treat the object with the same stewardship as they would treat their own property. Users pay a fee, based on duration and intensity of use (see Figure 8.3), and can assume that the object is safe to use. In cases of abuse, users can be excluded from the system.

In the analogue (non-digital) economy, rental goods had to be returned to the owner-fleet manager for control before another user would take over. This enabled a regular control and clear attribution of responsibility for damages and shortcomings (cleanliness, empty fuel tanks). 'Trust is fine, but control is better' is an old maxim in management and politics. Cultural differences from one user to the next do not pose a problem to fleet managers.

In a digital 'sharing Performance Economy', however, responsibilities are no longer straightforward (Stahel 2016). Autolib, a company in Paris managing a rental car system combining electric cars (low maintenance), reserved parking spaces equipped with recharging stations and an electronic reservation system, gave up in 2018. Despite the technical soundness of the concept, it failed economically because of a lack of control by the fleet manager, a lack of caring by users, vandalism and political quarrels. Mobike, a Chinese company renting bicycles with solid rubber wheels (no flat tyres to repair), which can be left anywhere and used spontaneously where they are (free float principle), has been banned in a number of cities (Zurich, Singapore, China) because of chaotic user behaviour and an absence of control by the owner-fleet manager. By contrast, in Oxford, a city dominated by academics and a caring tradition, several different rental bike systems (including Mobike) flourish in harmony.

The above are examples of innovative systems solutions developed by actors of the Performance Economy trying to marry analogue technology with the opportunities of the Internet of Things. But in contrast to the analogue 'sharing Performance Economy', these examples rely on exploiting the BIG DATA created by the users of the objects as source of income, not the rental income from the objects as such. But economic failure due to a cultural lack of caring by the users of the objects could not be prevented by the Internet of Things;

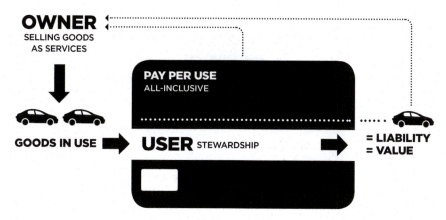

Figure 8.3 Singular ownership and shared responsibility in an analogue 'sharing economy'

the old economic paradigm 'if something is free, it has no value (and will be abused)' might be with us for ever.

In a digital 'sharing Performance Economy', ownership, income, liability and responsibility between the pro-user (you) and the fleet managers (owners of the objects and the IT systems tracking you) are fuzzy. In the centre of the action are no longer the objects as such, but 'BIG DATA' created by the user, and issues around data protection and data abuse (Figure 8.4).

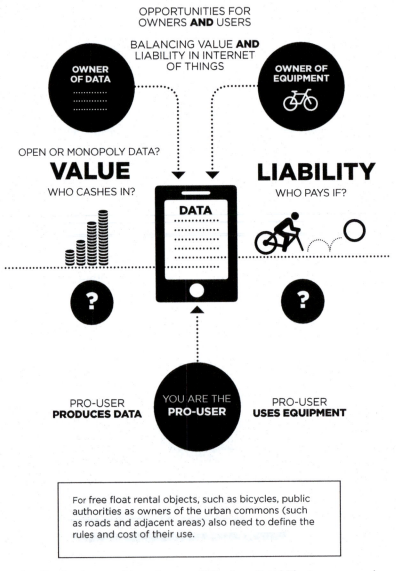

Figure 8.4 Confused ownership and responsibility in a digital 'sharing economy'

Policymakers will have to come to grips with the issues of authorship and intellectual property rights in the Internet of Things. The user is the producer and legal owner of the data he creates, similarly to a music composer or writer. Toffler defined the pro-sumer, or producer-consumer, in the linear industrial economy (Toffler 1980).[2] The identity and rights of the pro-user, or producer-user, in the Performance Economy is a much more complex issue, which still needs to be defined and protected by policymakers.

In the case of free float rental objects using public ground, such as bicycles, public authorities as owners of the urban commons (such as roads and adjacent areas) also need to define the rules and costs of their use.

The digitalisation of the economy, autonomous goods and the Internet of Things demand clear legal guidelines. For objects purchased by owner-users and connected to the Internet of Things, be it smartphones or John Deere tractors, the ownership-liability issue is fuzzy. In the case of smart vehicles, is the driver still liable for accidents? Ownership may be split between hardware (the producer and/or owner of the car) and software (the producer and/or owner of the algorithms driving the vehicle). Whose liability and property are smart goods: the producer-owner of the software,[3] the owner of the hardware or the user?

In a 'sharing society', without an explicit owner, the principle of 'no sharing without caring' also applies, exemplified by the Global Commons, such as atmosphere, oceans, biodiversity. In the absence of an owner, sharing without caring can lead to abuse and overexploitation without punishment, and ultimately the tragedy of the Commons. In closely knit communities, social shaming can be a form of punishment that leads to an exclusion from participating in a system or from being part of the community (Stahel 1997).

8.5 The foundation of the Performance Economy: the factor 'Time'

Nature has a timelessness given by the circularity of organic material, where waste becomes food. But this principal in nature does not apply to manufactured objects and materials in both the linear and the circular industrial economy; in the latter, concerted human motivation and determination is needed to close the physical loops of objects and materials at their highest value.

The wish to mitigate potential future catastrophic events led around 1800, after the first explosions of steam engines and dynamite factories, to the birth of risk management; DuPont de Nemours, producer of the 'DuPont Powder', is still a leader in risk management today. The modern comprehensive risk management thinking in Europe started after the Flixborough disaster in 1974, when a huge explosion ripped apart a chemical plant located on the banks of River Trent in Lincolnshire, UK. Twenty-eight people died, 53 were injured and the small town next to the plant was wrecked.

The objective of risk management is to balance opportunities and losses. The linear industrial economy is a technical system optimisation of technology and

risk management to increase the engineering efficiency of the production process – the left vertical plane of Figure 8.5.

Loss prevention as a key objective of risk management is also highly relevant
for the circular industrial economy and its objective of maintaining the value
and utility of stocks of manufactured objects and molecules. Adding the factor
'Time' as sustainability management to the technical system optimisation of the
industrial economy in Figure 8.5 has three effects:

- the Performance Economy as a three-dimensional optimisation issue;
- the addition of the two plains of utilisation optimisation and liability optimisation to the traditional techno-economic optimisation process;
- a new definition of Quality as the basis of the Performance Economy:
  selling performance as the vector of this triple optimisation.

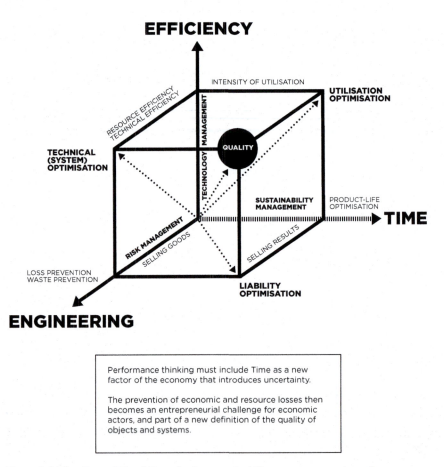

Figure 8.5 The factor 'Time', introducing sustainability management into the economy

Time introduces uncertainty into the economy: we cannot predict the future, but we can predict that the prevention of economic, human and resource losses becomes an entrepreneurial challenge for economic actors, not at least to reduce reputational risks, and part of a new definition of long-term quality.

Economy and ecology meet in sustainable business models with a long time horizon because waste prevention is also a prevention of economic loss! 'Zero waste' is thus also a business strategy; because catastrophic loss events, such as Schweizerhalle (Section 2.2), also lead to a considerable loss of reputation for the company.

8.6 Uncertainty, diseconomy of risk and economy of scale, resilience

The issue of time and uncertainty is very relevant in prevention activities: if there is no fire, prevention will be more expensive than doing nothing. This is why economists often question the productivity of prevention measures, which is difficult to estimate before a disaster happens. But in the long term, prevention always pays (Giarini and Stahel 1989).

The circular industrial economy is open-ended, whereas the linear industrial economy ends at the point of sale. Uncertainty and the risk of a loss increase over time for any hazard, and therefore gain in importance for the circular industrial economy.

The economy of scale of the linear industrial economy goes hand in hand with diseconomy of risk, but the latter is not taken into account in traditional economic optimisation. The incremental benefits of economy of scale diminish with size, whereas the catastrophic risk potential grows exponentially. If a manufacturer produces goods in one or two factories this has a small impact on the unit cost of production. But in case of a disaster, he loses 100 per cent of production capacity in the first case, and only 50 per cent in the second. It is therefore safe to say that the intelligent decentralisation inherent in the circular industrial economy is also an efficient loss prevention strategy.

Preventive maintenance of objects used in the Performance Economy is another example where prevention pays. If economic actors get paid only for results and have to guarantee the function or performance of their objects, preventive maintenance pays because it reduces the risk of a breakdown. Where the availability of, for instance, electricity is mission critical, such as in operating theatres of hospitals or for computers in surveillance and communication activities, strategies of redundancy and resilience become a necessity.

Redundancy means having spare equipment in stand-by mode: resilience means a system design which enables to rapidly return to normal life. Resilient cities are a major initiative in social sustainability, pioneered by the Rockefeller Foundation. The 100 resilient cities programme of the foundation helps cities around the world to become more resilient to the physical, social and economic challenges that are a growing part of the twenty-first century.[4] In-built resilience and redundancy thus are pillars of sustainable societies and are increased by the Performance Economy.

The Performance Economy of selling goods and molecules as a service is the most sustainable business model at the heart of the circular industrial economy because it:

- internalises the cost of product liability, risk and waste;
- saves transaction and compliance costs;
- increases profit opportunities by exploiting sufficiency and systems solutions, in addition to efficiency ones;
- contributes to corporate and national resource security.

If producers retain the ownership of their goods, the goods of today are tomorrow's resources at yesteryear's commodity prices, and increase the resilience of society through a future resource security.

Notes

1 Quasi-rental service activities are sometimes called sharing economy, platform economy (Uber, Airbnb, FlixBus) or Product-Service Systems (PSS), for reasons of brand distinctions more than strategic differences.
2 The term *prosumption* was coined by Alvin Toffler and refers to a combination of production and consumption, for example a customer creating the configuration of his PC to be produced by e.g. Dell.
3 For a number of reasons, including IPR, manufacturers like Apple and John Deere sell the hardware of technology systems (smartphones and tractors) but refuse to give their customers access to the source codes and algorithms of the software, which would enable them to repair the technical systems and control and extend their service-life.
4 Resilient Cities Project of the Rockefeller Foundation. 100 Resilient Cities was created by the Rockefeller Foundation on the foundation's Centennial in 2013. Work began with a first group of 32 cities in December of 2013. In 2014, a second cohort of 35 cities was announced. The third 100 Resilient Cities Challenge closed in November of 2015 and the final group of cities was announced in May 2016.

References

Giarini, Orio and Stahel, Walter R. (1989) *The limits to certainty, facing risks in the new service economy*. Kluwer Academic Publishers, Dordrecht.

Hagan, Andrew and Tost, Michael (2019) Metal leasing. A scientific paper submitted for publication in 2019.

Harvard Business School (1994) Xerox: Design for the environment. Case study N9–794–022, 7 January.

IFG Internationales Forum für Gestaltung (1993) *Gemeinsam nutzen statt einzeln verbrauchen, Eine neue Beziehung zu den Dingen (Common utilisation instead of singular consumption)*. Anabas Verlag, Giessen.

Resilient Cities Project of the Rockefeller Foundation (2013–today) New York. www.100resilientcities.org/, accessed 22 December 2018.

Stahel, Walter R. (1997) The service economy: Wealth without resource consumption? *Philosophical Transactions A*, vol. 355, pp. 1309–1319.

Stahel, Walter R. (2010) *The performance economy,* second edition. Palgrave Macmillan, Houndmills.

Stahel, Walter R. (2016) Beyond the 'triple helix'. EESD 2016 conference, Engineering Education for Sustainable Development, Bruges, 5 September. Conference proceedings.

Toffler, Alvin (1980) *The third wave.* Bantam Books, New York.

9 Radical innovation to enhance stock management

Radical innovation in stock management are components to upgrade existing systems and jumps in technology. Innovative components can be integrated into existing stocks through technologic or fashion upgrades; jumps in technology will lead to a gradual replacement of stocks and away grading of objects for reuse elsewhere, or dismantling to recover components or the recovery of molecules. The development of new molecules and technologies to recover molecules at a purity-as-new will need upfront investments in science and R&D.

9.1 The drivers of innovation in the circular industrial economy

In a mature circular industrial economy (Figure 9.1), production becomes a segment of the loop of the circular industrial economy, with the task of producing innovative components and objects to upgrade and renew the stocks of objects. In construction and the electro-mechanical world, technology upgrades often involve singular components, which can be replaced by new-tech components fulfilling the same function.

Radical technical innovation does often not depend upon a single scientific discipline or industrial sector. Recognising the potential of sleeping innovation will help speeding up their application in the market; this selection process is open to academia, industry, government authorities and other innovators.

If manufacturers refuse visible jumps in technology, preferring incremental innovation in order to prevent stranded capital, sudden change is programmed. Tesla versus the world car industry is a recent example of this. For the circular industrial economy, jumps in technology impact first the value and utility of the stock of objects, and are thus a hazard for actors of the era of 'R'. Second, they lead to an avalanche of used material in the era of 'D'. But these stock changes are foreseeable, slower and less abrupt than those hitting manufacturer flows.

A key driver of progress in the circular industrial economy has always been economics, the cost of service-life extension versus the price of similar new objects. Innovation that reduces the costs of repairs and spare parts (3D-Print) will boost the era of 'R'. High volatility in commodity prices and the cost of labour can be drivers or obstacles for the eras of 'R' and 'D'; policymakers with

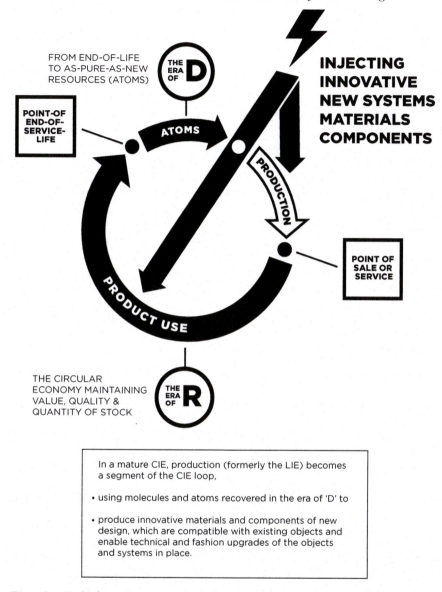

FROM END-OF-LIFE
TO AS-PURE-AS-NEW
RESOURCES (ATOMS)

THE ERA OF **D**

INJECTING INNOVATIVE NEW SYSTEMS MATERIALS COMPONENTS

POINT-OF-END-OF-SERVICE-LIFE

ATOMS

PRODUCTION

POINT OF SALE OR SERVICE

PRODUCT USE

THE CIRCULAR ECONOMY MAINTAINING VALUE, QUALITY & QUANTITY OF STOCK

THE ERA OF **R**

In a mature CIE, production (formerly the LIE) becomes a segment of the CIE loop,

- using molecules and atoms recovered in the era of 'D' to

- produce innovative materials and components of new design, which are compatible with existing objects and enable technical and fashion upgrades of the objects and systems in place.

Figure 9.1 Radical innovation in materials, components, systems

a vision of the future can directly influence both factors through, for example, taxation.

Science, by contrast, does not directly generate change. Global resource security became a topic after the 1973 research report on the 'Limits to growth' by the Club of Rome, which reached a worldwide audience but did not hit commodity prices. The concept of a circular industrial economy, which emerged a few years later (Stahel and Reday-Mulvey 1976), found no audience for some time despite the fact that it offered a solution to this perceived threat.

Innovation as a change agent is not limited to technology. Economic and financial research could also drive change, but has a high resistance to study radical changes, such as the circular industrial economy, which will question present academic wisdom. Remanufacturers know that the Return on Investment (ROI) in remanufacturing combustion engines is five times the ROI in manufacturing similar objects, but academia is hardly interested. The potential impact on the economic wellbeing of applying this knowledge to other sectors is un-researched.

Systemic innovation by industry could be a major change agent, but is slow. In 1992, reducing the resource consumption of industrialised countries by 90 per cent – a factor of ten – and analysing its implications for economy and society was proposed and analysed by the members of the Factor Ten Club. Publications on this research were successful but considered academic (Weizsäcker *et al.* 1995; Hawken *et al.* 1999).[1] In 2017, 25 years after its formulation, the Factor Ten concept has been adopted by the World Business Council of Sustainable Development (WBCS 2018).

9.2 Innovation in the era of 'R'

In the circular economy of necessity, efforts to maintain the utility of objects dominate; innovation often comes from craftsmen looking to produce new products from 'waste', transforming used objects into new ones, such as steel drums into kitchen ware (Papanek 1971).

The circular industrial economy in societies of abundance aims to maintain value and utility of objects, by developing cheaper 'R' technologies or new components allowing a technologic or fashion upgrade of objects.

If users had a voice and would be heard, they could become major change agent in the shift to a circular industrial economy. A 2014 survey found that 77 per cent of the citizens in the European Union would rather fix their products than buy new ones, and identified high costs and low availability of repair services as predominant barriers. Petitions in Germany, Italy and the UK asking for easily repairable and longer-lasting products were approaching 200,000 signatures in 2018.

Fleet managers in the Performance Economy have traditionally been among the key technical innovators, for economic reasons. Developing innovative low-maintenance, spare-less repair and remanufacture methods is the ultimate engineering challenge to minimise the operation and maintenance costs of a stock of objects, or to maximise profits in selling goods as a service. In the 1970s, the US Air Force developed a diffusion bonding technology to repair jet engine blades without the need for spare parts, and methods of cannibalising 'waste' aircraft to recover components as cheap spares.

When it started selling 'power by the hour', Rolls-Royce developed systems to monitor the condition and performance of engines during flight. This allowed them to pre-emptively address any maintenance issues with lower-cost 'on-wing' repairs which help further maximise revenues by keeping the engine in operational service. These methods prevent waste, maximise resource utilisation and provide other business benefits through aligning Rolls-Royce's objectives to that of its customers, but the need for more highly qualified people in service activities has to be factored into any overall financial savings of such approaches.

In vintage cars, mechanical distributors needing regular adjustments can be replaced by maintenance-free electronic ones. But exploiting these opportunities is not taught in schools, it needs experienced economic actors knowledgeable both in new technologies and the existing stock of objects, which are rare.

Jumps in technology application can be forced by policymakers through pull innovation, building markets through public procurement. Based on visions of a sustainable future, the economy can be motivated to develop in a desired direction. Witness Norway's decision to pull economic development towards a zero-carbon economy. As a consequence, a Norwegian shipping company asked industry in 2018 to submit tenders for zero-emission coastal express vessels powered by hydrogen and fuel cells. Boreal and Wärtsilä Ship Design picked up the challenge and agreed to develop hydrogen-powered ferries despite the fact that the technology does not yet exist. The ferry will be the first vessel of its kind worldwide (Ferry shipping news 2018), opening the gate to abandoning marine diesel engines in coastal shipping.

Transforming a mechanical typewriter into a Personal Computer (PC) does not make sense, but upgrading mechanical bicycles into e-bikes, by fitting wheel-integrated electric micro-motors and adding a battery, or transforming an original Jaguar E-type from the 1960s into an electric one, is feasible and doable. The converted electric E-type hit the headlines when Meghan and Prince Harry used it to drive off after their wedding.

Innovation changes markets. Economic actors of the linear industrial economy are moving into the Performance Economy when objects with long-life low-maintenance components, such as electric motors, replace maintenance-intensive combustion engines with gearboxes. As long-life low-maintenance components lead to longer-life objects, manufacturers start to seize the opportunity to sell goods as a service in order to retain market control.

In the original IT world, hardware and software could be upgraded separately: hardware items were routinely replaced by new more powerful and/or energy saving components; and software was periodically upgraded, often online, to make computer systems more resilient. New external hardware like printers and hard disks were mostly compatible with existing equipment like PCs. Owner-users could keep the PC therefore 'as is' for a long time as up-to-date stand-alone systems.

Ownership and control remained with the owner of the hardware and a software licence. This is still the case for isolated systems like dash-cams and portable GPS. But most connected systems in objects can no longer be repaired or upgraded by the owner or even repair experts, if the source code is retained by the manufacturer. The Internet of Things changes the linear industrial economy principle that ownership, liability and control for an object are transferred at the point of sale from the seller to the buyer. Non-technology issues such as ownership and the right to repair may move into centre stage of policymaking innovation in the era of 'R'.

9.3 Innovation in the era of 'D'

This is the sector of the circular industrial economy with the biggest potential for technical innovation and research. Recovering the stocks of atoms and molecules at their highest utility and value (purity) level for reuse is a necessity once the reuse and service-life-extension options of the era of 'R' have been exhausted.

This demands new sorting technologies and processes to separate mixed (household) waste into clean material fractions, to dismantle used objects into clean separate material fractions (into different alloys of the same metal, for example) and finally technologies to recover molecules and atoms as pure as virgin resources.

Research into reusing atoms and molecules also opens up new territories in basic sciences, such as developing reusable manufactured materials (see the example of the Cookson Group, p. 69). Questions like: 'can CO_2 emissions become a resource to produce new chemicals, and will this new carbon chemistry be able to compete with petro-chemistry?' may find an answer through scientific research. Using Carbon Capture and Storage (CCS) and Carbon Capture for Utilisation (CCU) to produce hydrogen is another research topic, studied in Norway.

Recovering stocks of atoms and molecules for reuse at their highest value and purity level is the objective. But the recovered molecules will be in competition with those from virgin sources. As commodity prices have a high volatility, but investments into new technology are fixed and have a long payback period, the question arises how research in the era of 'D' can be financed.

Sorting manufactured materials is a new problem for the economy, non-existent in mining. Innovative economic actors should be in the driver seat of the era of 'D', governments can support these activities by creating appropriate framework conditions. The reward will be patentable solutions to recover atoms and molecules. This is a playing field open to international competition, and the winner may take it all. The opportunities include:

- De-bonding molecules, such as to de-polymerise polymers, de-alloy metal alloys, de-laminate carbon and glass fibre laminates, de-vulcanize used tyres to recover rubber and steel, de-coat objects.

  Plasto, a Norwegian company producing equipment for fish farming, has started to take back end-of-service-life objects made of High-density

Polyethylene (HDPE) in order to re-process the material to produce new equipment.

- De-constructing high-rise buildings and major infrastructure. Spain has started to dismantle its Yecla de Yeltes dam, the largest de-construction project of its kind ever in Europe; after its 'green change' decision, Germany is faced with the problem of deconstructing its nuclear power stations.

In cases where no technology solutions are found for used materials, pressure will mount beginning-of-pipe, on producers of the linear industrial economy to look for alternative materials, such as self-destroying polymers, or change their business models. The circular industrial economy thus opens up a wealth of opportunities for radical innovation in business models and processes, in the eras of 'R' and 'D' as well as in basic scientific and technological innovation.

9.4 The role of policymakers in innovation

Since the 1990s, techno-economic research with environmental objectives has flourished in areas like Life-Cycle Analysis (LCA), which has a limited scope of 'Cradle-to-Grave' (ISO 14044:2006). Research over several service-lives, such as MIPS – Material Intensity Per unit of Service (Schmidt-Bleek 1994) – and the Factor Ten Club did not catch on at the time, possibly because the importance of the 'units of service' concept was difficult to understand for experts, and even more difficult to translate into policy.

Political interests to reduce end-of-pipe waste volumes guided academic research to look into the circular industrial economy, to find uses for wastes from the building or electronic industry in order to reduce overwhelming waste volumes. Research programmes such as Horizon 2020 in the EU have motivated researchers to look into ways to maintain value and utility, such as reusing building components (ongoing EU BAMB project; and research projects by ARUP Partners), rather than recovering building materials, for example as aggregate in concrete.

Policymakers with a holistic vision, such as zero-waste or a low-carbon economy, and the capability of identifying innovations in search of industrial applications, can exercise an important pull function through focused research programmes and procurement specifications. This latter has been the case for a long time for the US administration and most recently for Norway. In nation states where policies and the economy are interlinked, like the People's Republic of China, this approach may lead to even faster results.

Note

1 See the work of the Factor Ten Club and Institute. www.factor10-institute.org/, accessed 22 January 2019. A dematerialisation of industrialised countries by a factor of

ten (minus 90 per cent) was first suggested 25 years ago by the Factor Ten Club in order to achieve sustainable economic development worldwide by 2050.

References

Ferry Shipping News (2018) 8 February and 17 May. www.ferryshippingnews.com/, accessed 23 January 2019.

Hawken, Paul, Lovins, Amory and Lovins, Hunter (1999) *Natural capitalism*. Little Brown and Company, Boston.

ISO 14044:2006 (2006). Environmental management – life cycle assessment – requirements and guidelines. International Standardisation Organisation, Geneva.

Papanek, Victor (1971) *Design for the Real World: Human Ecology and Social Change,*. Bantam Books, New York, NY.

Schmidt-Bleek, Friedrich (1994) *Wieviel Umwelt braucht der Mensch? MIPS — Das Mass für ökologisches Wirtschaften*. Birkhäuser Verlag, Basel.

Stahel, Walter and Reday-Mulvey, Geneviève (1976) The potential for substituting manpower for energy. Report to the Commission of the European Communities, Brussels.

WBCS (2018) Factor 10 news. www.wbcsd.org/Programs/Circular-Economy/Factor-10/News/launching-Factor10, accessed 31 December 2018.

Weizsäcker, Ernst Ulrich von, Lovins, Amory and Lovins, Hunter (1995) *Factor four*. A report to the Club of Rome. Droemer Knaur, Munich.

10 Outlook

An honest quest for holistic solutions to reach the SDGs will inevitably lead to a promotion of the shift to a circular industrial economy. Governments of industrialised countries should have a considerable self-interest in this shift also as protection against future government liability claims. The trends of a technology-driven 'New Economy' and regional strategies based on cultural identity and motivation may be the most powerful levers for change.

10.1 The circular industrial economy needs holistic approaches

In Autumn 2018, Dr Marcia McNutt, President of the U.S. National Academy of Sciences, reflected on lessons learned from the battle in the 1980s to protect the Earth's ozone layer. She noted that scientists had been saying for years that chlorofluorocarbons (CFCs) were destroying the ozone layer. But it took practical solutions to generate the widespread support needed to phase out CFCs. The lesson?

Evidence might be there, but unless there's a practical solution, the science will be ignored.

Today, scientists agree that the accumulation of large amounts of greenhouse gases in the Earth's atmosphere is slowly raising the global temperature and disrupting climate patterns, with worldwide economic implications.[1]

If we agree that anthropogenic CO_2 emissions are at least partly to blame for rising global temperature, then – with regard to industrialised countries – we have known the practical solution for several decades: to shift from a linear to a circular industrial economy, to manage the stocks of manufactured assets, instead of managing flows to replace existing assets with new clone assets.

Dr McNutt's statement is valid for the era of 'D', where practical solutions are missing for many challenges, but it does not apply to the era of 'R'. The most efficient strategy for policymakers is therefore to strongly support economic activities in the era of 'R', a rapid strategy that may trigger structural changes in the linear industrial economy. When science will yield practical results in the era of 'D', a second policy option will open but many precious years might be lost between consensus and decisive action.

Bold action from individuals, economic actors and policymakers is needed to do this. Self-motivation can help, remember Charlie Brown's 'You can do it, Charlie Brown!', or Roger Federer's 'Come on!' in critical situations on the tennis court. However, normal people need, and would greatly benefit from:

- 'figureheads' pointing the direction to go,[2] and lighthouses warning of hazards;
- information on 'how can I do it';
- motivation policies promoting Saint-Exupéry's longing for the sea, which are missing in today's techno-scientific discussions of the circular economy.

Figureheads are leading 'all on board', for instance in a given cultural context such as language. Translating existing wisdom – the best circular economy texts are in English – can be a key lever, such as the Institut de l'Environnement et de l'Économie Circulaire, founded in 2016 as joint organisation of three Montréal academic institutions and the government of Quebec, Canada, which helps raising the level of awareness for the opportunities of the circular industrial economy in French-speaking regions. Figureheads can also be regional political leaders with a clear vision, such as Dr Nicola Sturgeon, First Minister of Scotland, who proclaimed 'I want Scotland to be a real pioneer of Circular Economy', when opening the Circular Economy Hotspot Scotland in Glasgow on 31 October 2018.

Lighthouses have no cultural borders; they serve any ship passing by. They either guide ships to a safe harbour – the famous 'Pharos of Alexandria' – or warn them of hidden hazards, such as the lighthouse at Fastnet rock. Policymakers can have lighthouse functions, such as Dr Janez Potočnik, a Slovenian politician who served first as European Commissioner for Science & Research (2004–2010). In a second mandate, as European Commissioner for Environment (2010–2014), he prepared the EU Circular Economy Package, a fundamental piece of legislation. Tirelessly, he continues his engagement for a sustainable planet and today serves as Co-Chair of the UN International Resource Panel (IRP). But lighthouses can be ignored; decisions are taken by the captain of each ship, who may ignore warnings or advice on directions and not change course.

Information on 'how to do it' has many faces, as there is no single circular economy solution that fits all. This book has focused on manufactured objects and materials in a circular industrial economy of abundance and what individuals like YOU and me can do to adapt their daily life; what options economic actors willing to shift their business models to a circular industrial or Performance Economy as default option have; and some of the options policymakers and government have.

Policies have to be put into practice by politicians. When Anders Wijkman, co-president of the Club of Rome and former Member of the European

Parliament, presented his 2016 research report 'The circular economy and benefits for society: Jobs and climate are clear winners' to European politicians and policymakers, they hardly budged. Yet the report shows that a shift to the circular industrial economy in European countries will reduce national CO_2 emissions by 66 per cent and increase national employment by about 4 per cent, two topics which are high on any political agenda.

Megatrends outside the industrial mainstream, supporting the circular industrial economy, are many, for instance:

- the urgency of scientific reports on the impacts of climate change by the International Panel on Climate Change, NOAA and others, calling for immediate action;
- the shrinking number of countries willing to act as waste dumps for others, led by the People's Republic of China;
- calls for a shift from the current 'collective producer responsibility' framework to one of individual corporate accountability, even liability.

10.2 Governments: the elephant in the circular menagerie

National governments should have a major interest in accelerating the shift towards a circular industrial economy in order to:

- increase national resilience against potential trade wars and resource boycotts, as well as increase the national resource security through the resource stocks embodied in manufactured objects;
- use the local job creation potential, which includes silver workers and vocational training opportunities for the unskilled;
- exploit its huge domestic CO_2 compensation potential: its activities correspond to the characteristics of domestic Clean Development Mechanism (CDM) projects, which was a bone of contention at the COP 24;[3] and
- avoid potential climate change liability claims against governments in future.

The notion of a government liability could be the black swan driver hidden in the climate change topic (Taleb 2007). Ten years ago, some people in Geneva discussed suing the governments that had signed the 1997 Kyoto Protocol, but not fulfilled their promise, for 'abandoning a planet in distress'. The idea was not pursued for a lack of court to file the claim. Since 2015, similar actions have been undertaken in the United States and the Netherlands, the latter ending with a condemnation of the Dutch government. In summer 2018, 'protect the Planet' attacked the European Union for violation of the European Union's Charter of Fundamental Rights (*Die Zeit* 2018); in December 2018, several French NGOs[4] attacked the French government under the European Convention on Human Rights, for not protecting the French population against the health impact of climate change and for violating its climate engagements signed at COP 21 in Paris.

10.3 A technology-driven New Economy supports the circular industrial economy

The circular industrial economy is supported by, and part of, a new techno-economic development, which includes trends for:

- an intelligently decentralised economy;
- systems solutions; and
- long-life technologies leading to long-life objects.

Intelligent decentralisation: the emergence of industry 4.0, industrial robots and additive manufacturing (3-D print equipment) have promoted re-shoring and regional production workshops and led to a reindustrialisation of Europe and North America. Micro-breweries and bakeries as well as organic farming for local markets are other examples of this trend.

System solutions: Vacuum Insulation Panels (VIPs) are composite objects with a thermal conductivity ten times lower than common insulation materials; applications are wall insulation panels for houses and equipment, and windows. Window panes and frames are much thinner than in traditional components, greatly reducing material input, but needing more care in use.

An 'eDumper' is the biggest battery-driven electric vehicle worldwide. It operates in a quarry in Péry, Switzerland, transports 65 tonnes of material from an uphill quarry to a cement factory downhill. Each downhill trip under load charges the batteries and enables it to drive back uphill empty – an energy self-sufficient vehicle.

Long-life low-maintenance technologies lead to long-life objects. Electric motors have a technical life of 100 years. New generations of electric cars and trains powered by long-life hydrogen-fuel cells are low-carbon and on the market; trucks and coastal vessels will next be commercialised by 2020 in several countries.

10.4 The quest for holistic solutions

Could convinced politicians formulate new policies resulting in Saint-Exupéry's longing for the sea? Maybe telling people that the COP 21 objectives could be achieved by a policy shift in favour of a circular economy, without charging carbon taxes, would convince people to change their behaviour and search their happiness in the reuse and repairs of their belongings, realising that they do not have to renounce what they have but change the way they use it?

The biggest lever to push the circular industrial economy to the forefront may be a general perception that most of the topics jeopardising world society, listed as the objectives of the UN Sustainable Development Goals – for instance carbon emissions, overconsumption of natural resources, unsustainable use (not consumption) of manufactured objects, work conditions and resource use inefficiency – could be tackled simultaneously by the shift to a circular industrial economy.

The plan to do it would need to be adapted to regional cultural issues, keeping in mind that industrially less developed regions, where improving food, health and education are priority needs for society, still need to build stocks of infrastructure and manufactured objects.

10.5 Culture, information and motivation: regional change levers

Sufficiency, not buying a new car, phone or garment even if new goods are more fashionable than what one has, needs information and motivation. As with climate change, the information is there but a convincing marketing is missing. Wearing second-hand clothes is the best strategy to protect especially infants against allergies. Garments which are allergy-free because they have been washed many times are available in second-hand and rental shops, or handed down within families. But few people are queueing up to buy second-hand clothing and most shops do not offer them.

Selling the performance of goods instead of the goods themselves lets fashion-conscious citizens continue to enjoy the use of objects with the freedom of frequent changes, but without causing premature waste and without top-down legislation. Other citizens may be attracted by sustainable approaches of a non-monetary nature, such as a sharing society and societal self-help groups. Repair cafés, where owners of broken goods regularly meet volunteers with repair knowledge and tools are examples of a sustainable sharing society or circular barter economy, as are local exchange markets of used objects. Knowledge and objects are treated here as a new Commons, no money changes hands.

Cultural heritage and personal identity can also play an important role in preserving objects. Society is as wasteful with knowledge as it is with goods and resources; can we restore the old wisdom of 'old is resourceful'? Events involving vintage cars or historic airplanes attract large crowds everywhere but do not seem to inspire people to do the same.

The business models of the Performance Economy strengthen the factor Time in the circular industrial economy, and increase its resilience to uncertainty by promoting a sustainable society.

The scientific evidence and a practical solution are there, referring back to Dr McNutt, so the challenge is to spread the knowledge to other economic sectors and geographic regions. In some cases, the issue of ownership versus stewardship, of German versus Roman law, may be a cultural obstacle. Ownership includes the right to destroy an object, stewardship demands to find the best reuse (Giarini 1980). In a society of abundance, legislation imposing a stewardship obligation to maintain the highest value and utility of goods could nevertheless lead to radical changes in behaviour.

A circular industrial economy is not the only smart and green strategy there is, but probably the most sustainable business model improving simultaneously ecologic, social and economic factors. Coming back to Saint-Exupéry's call: maybe moving the legal gateposts in favour of the Performance Economy, promoting the circular industrial economy as default option for a sustainable economy, is the best strategy policymakers have to create the longing for the sea?

The common denominator of these concepts may be a return to old-fashioned values, such as good husbandry and an attitude of caring rather than efficiency and productivity. This book has structured and illustrated the principles of the circular industrial economy but may not have answered the question of how to create '*la pente vers la mer*', the longing for the sea, mentioned by Antoine de Saint-Exupéry in Citadelle (Saint-Exupéry 1948).

If industrialised countries want to succeed in building a sustainable society, the foremost task is to create a longing for circularity, for a circular industrial economy, for instance by motivating today's shopping addicts to become reuse and repair addicts for their belongings, and good stewards for objects they rent or share.

The circular industrial economy is a bag full of opportunities and chances; we have to open the bag and motivate people to seize the opportunities. It will be achieved when figureheads like the First Minister of Scotland can proclaim: 'We, Scotland, are a circular economy'.

And my last words will be: 'We, the people, are the circular economy'!

We need to motivate and convince politicians through scientific information, individuals through culturally founded and regionally appropriate marketing. Motivating economic actors to change course may be best done by pioneers leading the example, like the late Ray Anderson, CEO of Interface, who in the 1990s pursued the goal of zero waste for his company and served some time as co-chair of the President's Council on Sustainable Development during President Clinton's administration.

The author is convinced that the circular economy is one of the paths to a sustainable future. Finding regional strategies corresponding to regional culture and leading to a sustainable world society in a holistic sense is a challenging task.

Notes

1 Quoted by Richard G. Newell, President and CEO, Resources for the Future, Christmas 2018.
2 A figurehead is a carved wooden decoration found at the prow of 'man of wars', the wooden warships of the second half of the second millennium.
3 At the Conference of Parties, COP 21 meeting 2015 in Paris, almost all governments present agreed on the necessity to reduce GHG emission in order to limit global warming to 2°C by 2030. The COP 24 meeting in Kattowice, Poland, in December 2018, showed that hardly any government had implemented actions to achieve this goal.
4 Greenpeace, Oxfam, l'association Notre affaire à tous, and Fondation pour la Nature et pour l'Homme. L'État français va faire l'objet d'un recours en justice pour action insuffisante contre le réchauffement climatique par plusieurs ONG plaignantes, qui ont adressé lundi un document préalable en ce sens au président Emmanuel Macron et au gouvernement français.

References

Die Zeit (2018) Missliche Lage. 30 August, no. 36, p. 31.

Giarini, Orio (1980) *Dialogue on wealth and welfare, an alternative view of world capital formation*. A report to the Club of Rome. Pergamon Press, Oxford.

Saint-Exupéry, Antoine (1948) *Citadelle*. Gallimard, Paris.

Taleb, Nicholas (2007) *The black swan*. Random House, New York.

Index